With scholarly insights and lucid writing, Craig Evans delves into biblical history to unlock answers to questions all of us have. Once again, he hits a home run!

—Lee Strobel, best-selling author of
The Case for Christ and *The Case for Grace*

God Speaks is insightful and easy to understand. It will help you answer today's tough questions rooted deep in Christianity's history.

—Jay Sekulow, Chief Counsel,
American Center for Law and Justice

GOD

SPEAKS

GOD

What He Says

SPEAKS

What He Means

CRAIG A. EVANS, PhD

WORTHY®
PUBLISHING

Published by Worthy Books, an imprint of Worthy Publishing Group, a division of Worthy Media, Inc., One Franklin Park, 6100 Tower Circle, Suite 210, Franklin, TN 37067.

WORTHY is a registered trademark of Worthy Media, Inc.

HELPING PEOPLE EXPERIENCE THE HEART OF GOD

eBook available wherever digital books are sold.

Library of Congress Cataloging-in-Publication Data

Evans, Craig A.
    God speaks : what he says, what he means / Dr. Craig Evans.
       pages cm
    Includes bibliographical references.
    ISBN 978-1-61795-481-8 (tradepaper)
    1. Bible--Criticism, interpretation, etc. I. Title.
    BS538.E93 2015
    220.1--dc23
                                2015003373

For foreign and subsidiary rights, contact rights@worthypublishing.com

ISBN: 978-1-61795-481-8 (softcover)

Published in association with Ted Squires Agency, Nashville, TN, tedsquires.com

Font: OnO Display. © David Engelby (via DaFont.com)
Cover Design: Knail, LLC (Kent Jensen)
Interior Design and Typesetting: Bart Dawson

Printed in the United States of America
15 16 17 18 19 RRD 8 7 6 5 4 3 2 1

For Don and Diane

Contents

Foreword

by Mark Burnett and Roma Downey

OUR WORLD TODAY needs to hear the message of the Bible more than ever. Although this marvelous book remains a best seller in the West and a much-sought-after book elsewhere in the world, its message strangely remains misunderstood or unheard by the vast majority of people. This is a great tragedy and it must be addressed.

This is why in recent years we have invested a great deal of our time and resources in the production of *The Bible*, the miniseries that aired in March 2013; *The Son of God*, released in cinemas the following year; and *A.D. The Bible Continues*, which aired in 2015. But to produce these films was not something that we could do on our own. It was not something that could be done by drawing upon the usual resources and talents one finds in Hollywood.

To produce the story of the Bible for television viewers, it was necessary to tap into the knowledge of historians, archaeologists, and Bible experts from around the world. We consulted with experts in Greek and Hebrew (the original languages of the Bible), with archaeologists and experts in the study of the Holy Land (where the events recorded in the Bible took place), and Jewish and Christian experts in the interpretation of the Bible. Their input was invaluable and was a major factor in the success of *The Bible* miniseries, which was viewed by more than one hundred million people.

One of the experts we consulted with is Dr. Craig Evans, professor of New Testament at Acadia University in Nova Scotia, Canada. Dr. Evans has published more than seventy books on the Bible. He visits the land of Israel regularly and has participated in archaeological excavations in Jerusalem, Galilee, and elsewhere. He has taught courses on Jesus and the Gospels for more than thirty-five years and has appeared as an expert commentator on many television documentaries and news programs. We were delighted that he was willing to assist us in the writing and production of our programs.

We were also delighted to hear that Dr. Evans has written *God Speaks: What He Says, What He Means.* This book puts into written form what we have tried to convey cinematically. *God Speaks* clearly and concisely presents the message and relevance of the Bible in a way that all readers will enjoy and benefit from.

This book explores and explains all of the important issues relating to the Bible, provides important historical and archaeological evidence that shows the Bible is indeed a book of truth, and at the same time is easy to read. Through the pages of *God Speaks,* all will come to understand the message of the Bible in a deeper and fresher way.

Introduction

THE PURPOSE OF THIS BOOK is to invite you to take up the Bible and begin reading it with new eyes, seeing things that you have not seen before. My hope is that you will recognize that the Bible is not an old book full of myths that no longer have meaning, but rather it is a timeless book whose life-changing truths speak to every generation.

The Bible is the world's all-time best-seller, a shaper of Western culture and society, yet today most people are unaware of its life-changing message. Many people think the Bible is irrelevant today because they don't know what it is or what it says. I have heard people say things like, "The Bible is an old book. What makes it special, and why should I be guided by it?"

It's a strange attitude to have, if you think about it. The teachings of the Bible have lifted the standard of living in the West to levels that have never been enjoyed before in the history of the human race. Yet, most modern people do not stop to think why that is. If the Bible is an old, irrelevant book, then how could it have had such a powerful impact for good? If the Bible is little more than myth and superstition, then how do we explain the powerful role it has played in promoting literacy, education, and scientific progress? Why is it, then, that everywhere the Bible's message and teaching have been embraced, society is much better off? If the Bible has nothing to offer, then how did the West, where historically the Bible has been taken seriously, leap past the East, where the Bible has until recent times found little reception?

Any fair reading of history will show that the Bible has been a powerful force for progress and the betterment of the human race. Concepts such as justice, charity, human rights, humane treatment of animals, and respect for nature itself are all rooted in the Bible's teaching. We often think of the Ten Commandments, which, among other things, prohibit murder, theft, and perjury. Yet this is only a small sampling of what the Bible teaches. In the New Testament the Bible underscores the importance of love and forgiveness and promotes a form of egalitarianism that we moderns find surprisingly current and ahead of its time. Maybe this old book—the Bible—is not irrelevant after all.

The Bible not only transforms society, but it also transforms individuals. Here we are on more familiar ground. Everyone has heard stories of people whose lives have been changed for the better; people who have embraced the message of the Bible and have gone from despair and ruin to redemption and a new lease on life. What is it about the Bible that produces such transformation? How can an old book, whose message and teachings are supposedly out of date, have such a powerful and positive impact on people?

God Speaks: What He Says, What He Means answers these questions. The message of the Bible transforms lives and changes society because of the divine Author who stands behind its message. The Bible is no mere compilation of opinions and imagination. At the very center of the Bible is God who speaks. And what he says directly applies to every one of us. The message of the Bible is a *personal* message. It is a message that speaks to you and me. This is why we should care about the Bible. It is much more than an old book, filled with outdated ideas and strange beliefs. Far from it. It is a book whose message is as fresh, compelling, and transformational as it was when it was written long, long ago. Most homes in America have Bibles in them. It's time to start reading them.

But not everyone will agree with me. In the last decade or so we have witnessed the rise of what is called the New Atheism, in which faith in God is decried and ridiculed with an energy and vehemence not seen before.[1] The Bible itself is often targeted. One Internet blogger has asserted: "The Bible and the people who produced it were barbaric and superstitious." The same blogger assures his readers: "The Bible is irrelevant to modern scientifically literate people."[2] A professor in one of the universities in my province recently remarked in public: "Religion is a horrid thing."[3]

A lot of people accept at face value such negative judgments. Even Christians themselves do not always know how to respond. It isn't because they lack the necessary skills for engaging in debate; they often don't know the Bible itself very well. Part of the problem is that what the Bible actually teaches—in contrast to the caricatures offered by comedians and outspoken atheists—is simply not known. Other then a few familiar platitudes people simply do not know what the Bible says.

A generation ago most people living in the Western world were familiar with the great figures and themes of the Bible. People knew who Abraham and Moses were, knew the story of the Israelites, the Exodus, and the Promised Land; and they certainly knew who Jesus of Nazareth was. Until fifty years ago most children learned and prayed the Lord's Prayer and recited the Ten Commandments. Allusions to well-known biblical phrases and personalities were commonplace in everyday life. Most people knew what Christmas and Easter were all about. Society generally embraced the Judeo-Christian worldview. Indeed, practically everyone knew that the very calendar itself is based upon the birth of Jesus.

Today's world, however, is very different. Most people outside the Church haven't a clue what the Bible is and what it says. They may have vague ideas about Jesus, but they have little knowledge of the Bible's message. In recent years people on the street have been asked about the origins of Christmas and Easter. Very few could speak intelligently about these important holy days.

Not only is the content of the Bible not well understood, its origins and its history of transmission and translation are not well understood either. This ignorance makes it easy for books like Dan Brown's *The Da Vinci Code* and other books that are filled with errors and misleading claims about the Bible and its origins to gain a wide hearing.

But it is not only people's ignorance of the Bible that concerns me; it is the frequent misrepresentation of the Bible's message in today's increasingly militant atheism and anti-Christian polemic. Have you heard critics who say something like this: "The Bible is violent, chauvinist, racist, and immoral. It is little more than a collection of irrelevant stories and myths"? Comments like these have become all too common.

Often the principal objection to the Bible is that this ancient book is focused on God. And belief in God—according to atheists—is not a good thing. Belief in God, so they say, leads to extremism, division, intolerance, and violence. Islamic terrorism is usually cited as evidence for the truth of these claims. Accordingly, humanity would be better off ignoring the Bible and no longer believing in God. So goes the argument.

I believe this argument is profoundly flawed and misguided. The message of the Bible is all about God's love for humanity. It is not strange at all that the best-known Bible verse begins with the words, "For God so loved the world . . . " (John 3:16). The message of the Bible is a message of love, reconciliation, redemption, and transformation. It is a message of forgiveness and hope, a message that brings humans together and brings them into a restorative relationship with God, the Creator of the universe, a message that resonates in the hearts of hearers.

Today our world is marked by anger, despair, moral relativity, and shocking violence. In the eyes of many there simply is no right and no wrong. Indeed, some go so far as to claim that there really is no purpose to human life. We are nothing more than a biological fluke, we are told. Those who hold to this dismal worldview have little to offer. The atheist experiments, seen especially in the Communism of the former Soviet Union and other nations, have been dismal failures, not only with respect to economy but especially so with respect to the treatment of their citizens. The human rights records of these "officially atheist" regimes are appalling. It is hard to avoid concluding that the more society pushes God out of the picture the more society sinks into dehumanizing relativity.

The message of the Bible stands in stark contrast with the messages of those who think God no longer has anything to offer or that Christian faith is passé. The Bible speaks compellingly of God's love for humanity. It provides a moral compass and a sure guide for all that we face in life. In the pages that follow I want to describe what the Bible offers us, to make as clear as possible its message of love, reconciliation, and hope.

* * *

God Speaks: What He Says, What He Means is divided into three parts. Part 1 deals with the basics, asking what the Bible really is and what the Bible really says. This part will orient you to all that follows. Most readers will be quite surprised when they discover what the Bible is (it really isn't a book!) and what it says (it really isn't full of dos and don'ts!).

Part 2 inquires into what the Bible is all about. Among other things, we look at the story of creation, the ancient laws of Moses, the Bible's promises, and the consequences of ignoring what the Bible says. You will discover that the creation story does not require you to ignore science, that the laws of Moses are not oppressive, and that the consequences of ignoring what the Bible teaches are pretty serious.

In part 2 we also will look at Jesus: where he came from, what he taught, and why he is so important. Once again you will be surprised. You will find that Jesus was no namby-pamby. On the contrary, Jesus was a man's man who stood up for the poor and weak and confronted the powerful and the rich. You will also find out why the resurrection of Jesus is no myth.

In Part 3 we shall consider a number of very important questions. These include how we interpret the Bible, how we are to understand the violence in the Bible, what light discoveries shed on the Bible, as well as when things that the Bible talks about happened. What you will find out is that the interpretation of the Bible involves serious study. It is no fly-by-the-seat-of-your-pants process. You actually do have to know what you are doing, every bit as much as any historian of antiquity needs to know what he or she is doing. But you will also discover that accurate interpretation of the Bible is possible and that there are plenty of tools that can help you understand the Bible.

I think you will find very interesting the many discoveries that have been made that show that the Bible really does describe things that happened. For example, the Gospels that tell us about Jesus actually are reliable and there is compelling evidence that supports this claim. Believing what the Bible says about Jesus does not require "blind faith"; just an inquiring mind that is open to the evidence.

An inquiring mind is all that is required to get the full benefit of *God Speaks*. This book has been written for those who seek truth and not confirmation for bias and unsupported opinion. Do you really want to know what the Bible says? What God has spoken? If you do, then *God Speaks* was written for you.

Part One

WHAT IS THE BIBLE?

1

What Is the Bible, Really?

MOST PEOPLE WHO DISMISS the Bible as an old, irrelevant book—little more than a collection of religious opinions from a bygone era—either haven't read it or haven't understood it. In most cases, they are reacting to comments and ideas they have heard from other people who haven't read the Bible with understanding. I even know someone who bases his opinion of what the Bible teaches on what he sees on the television cartoon *The Simpsons*! That would be funny if it weren't so sad.

In this book, I will give you a solid, easy-to-understand guide to the Bible. I begin with the basics, so that you will get the big picture of what the Bible really *is*. In the next chapter we will look at some important, specific issues, so that you will get a much better idea of what the Bible really *says*. When you discover what it is and what it says, you will see why this "old book" is so important.

> The Bible is a small but very important library.

What is the Bible? The word *Bible* means *book*. At first glance that seems obvious. Of course it is a book. But is it? In reality the Bible is a small but very important library made up of (at least) sixty-six books—thirty-nine in the Old Testament (the first part of the Bible) and twenty-seven in the New Testament (the second part of the Bible). Roman Catholics, Greek Orthodox, and other Eastern Christians include in the Old Testament several other books called the Apocrypha, so their book count is higher.[1] In all, there were some forty authors who contributed to the Bible over the course of about fifteen hundred years.

The Old Testament is the Jewish Bible (sometimes called the Hebrew Bible, because it is written in the Hebrew language). The New Testament is the part that Christians—followers of Jesus— wrote. Although some early Christians thought the New Testament alone was sufficient as the Bible of the Church, the great majority of Christian leaders disagreed, believing that the Church's Bible should consist of *both* the Old Testament and the New Testament.

It was the right decision because the Old Testament provides the context and framework for understanding the New Testament. In other words, the New Testament wouldn't make sense to us without the Old Testament.

The Old Testament tells the story of God's good creation, what went wrong, and how God set in motion a plan to set things right again. Perhaps the most famous couple is Adam and Eve, who are depicted as the first human beings. They are also the most controversial. Many conservative literalists read the story of Adam and Eve and their children (Genesis 1–4) the way they read history. Taking the same literalistic approach to the creation story as a whole, some conservative readers believe it is necessary to reject the findings of science, claiming, instead, that planet Earth is only six or seven thousand years old.

But many Christian scholars and scientists believe that the early chapters of Genesis represent metaphor or parable. The story of creation intends to teach that the world is not the result of blind chance but rather the result of design and intention. So also humanity. However old the earth is, at some point and in some way God created human beings. The ancient stories of Genesis do not represent modern science (which to ancient people would have been incomprehensible) but the great truths that the world is not an accident and that humans are much more than sophisticated animals. Genesis also teaches that the problems humans face are largely brought upon themselves. The story of the fall of Adam and Eve teaches that humanity is inclined to go its own way, often to its own hurt.

The fallenness of humanity, however, does not mean that humans cannot be good or moral. Indeed they can. After all, Genesis teaches that God created humans in his own image (Genesis 1:26). This means that humans are both intelligent and moral. As a result, all humans have a moral code, in which all of us agree that some things are wrong and other things are right. Nevertheless, because we struggle to find our way morally and ethically and because we often choose to ignore God, we harm ourselves in one way or another.

As bad as this sounds, God has not given up on humanity. In response to humanity's fall, God has set in motion a plan to redeem and restore. The plan begins with God choosing an elderly couple, Abraham and Sarah, who miraculously have a son in their old age and become a family. This family becomes a people. This people becomes a nation—the nation of Israel. From Israel rise prophets, priests, and kings. The voices of these prophets, the ministry of these priests, and the rule of these kings create a framework through which we understand the New Testament.

The unfinished story of hope in the Old Testament reaches its climax in the pages of the New Testament, beginning with the miraculous birth of another son—God's Son, Jesus, in whom the whole story of the Old Testament finds its fulfillment. Jesus' life without sin; his ministry of miracles; his passion and death; and his resurrection, ascension, and promised reign are all properly understood in the light of the story of Abraham's descendants and the covenant family God created—a family of which, through Jesus, we all may become part.

What we call the Old Testament was Jesus' Bible. He respected it and accepted its authority. Without the Old Testament we would not effectively understand the message of Jesus. Make no mistake about it: the Old Testament is a vital part of the Bible.

The Old Testament, The First Part of the Bible

Some of the Old Testament books date to about 1000 BC (and portions of the oldest books could be earlier). Most of the books range from about 450 BC to 800 BC. The most recent is the book of Daniel, which is usually dated around 165 BC (although the stories in Daniel are probably much older). If you include the books of the Apocrypha, then some are more recent, dating to the first century BC.[2]

The Old Testament is made up of the books of Moses (Genesis, Exodus, Leviticus, Numbers, and Deuteronomy), a number of historical narratives (such as Joshua, Judges, 1–2 Samuel, 1–2 Kings), prophets (Isaiah, Jeremiah, etc.) and poetic writings (Psalms, Proverbs, Ecclesiastes, and the like). The historical narratives are sometimes called the "Former Prophets" and the books of Isaiah, Jeremiah, Ezekiel, and the twelve Minor Prophets (Hosea–Malachi) are called the "Latter Prophets." First and Second Chronicles and the book of Daniel are included in a category called the "Writings."

How these various writings are arranged varies somewhat from tradition to tradition.³

Most of the Old Testament books were written in Hebrew. Half of the book of Daniel and a few portions of other books were written in Aramaic, a language that is close to Hebrew. The people of Israel spoke Hebrew. After the Babylonians conquered Israel in the sixth century BC, many Jews spoke Aramaic, which is why two of the later books (Daniel and Nehemiah) have bits of Aramaic text.

In antiquity the Old Testament was translated into Greek and Latin. The Greek Orthodox Church uses the Greek version, while for centuries the Roman Catholic Church used the Latin version. The Eastern Orthodox Church reads a Syriac version of the Bible. (Syriac is a later form of Aramaic.) Most Christians, of course, read the Old Testament in their native language, whether English, French, German, Spanish, or whatever. Almost all of these modern language translations are based on the original languages of the Old Testament.

No other book has influenced Western culture more than the Old Testament. Adam and Eve in the Garden of Eden, Noah and the Flood, Moses and the Ten Commandments, Samson and Delilah, David and Goliath, David and Bathsheba, Daniel and the lions, and many other characters and stories have left a lasting impression in art, film, literature, and popular culture. It may be a very old collection of writings, but the Old Testament's influence is still strongly felt today.

The New Testament, The Second Part of the Bible

The New Testament books date from about AD 50 to AD 100. The New Testament is made up of four Gospels (Matthew, Mark,

Luke, and John), which provide accounts of the life, teaching, and activities of Jesus Christ; a historical narrative called the book of Acts, which describes the first generation or so of the early Church (from Jesus in AD 30 to Paul's journey to Rome in AD 62); several letters (many of them by Paul); and the Apocalypse, or book of Revelation.[4] Whereas most of the Old Testament books are written in Hebrew, the New Testament books are written in Greek.

The New Testament has also impacted our culture in major ways. We speak of a "good Samaritan" who renders assistance to someone in need. We refer to a "prodigal" who has seen the error of his ways. People speak of "turning the other cheek" and the Golden Rule's admonition that we do to others what we expect them to do to us. Most of us have heard the Lord's Prayer ("Our Father, who is in heaven . . .") or at least some of the Beatitudes ("Blessed are the poor in spirit . . ."). All these expressions and themes come from the teaching of Jesus. One of the best-known chapters in the New Testament is 1 Corinthians 13, a passage on love often read at weddings: "Love is patient and kind. . . . Love bears all things, believes all things, hopes all things, endures all things."

> It is not enough simply to have a Bible. We need to read it and understand it.

The teaching of Jesus and his disciples inspired movements that called for the end of slavery, equality for women, and the establishment of schools, hospitals, orphanages, and countless charities dedicated to assisting the poor and vulnerable. Characters, events, and themes from the New Testament are widely reflected in art and literature.

Together, the Old and New Testaments make up the Bible, the

most important library of ancient books ever assembled. But it is not enough simply to have a Bible. We need to read it and understand it.

Interpreting Scripture

Learning how to interpret Scripture is important and rewarding. Everyone needs a little help too. You will learn how to interpret Scripture, step by step, in chapter 10 of this book. You will also find many helpful resources listed under "For Further Reading." I can't emphasize enough the importance of proper, informed interpretation. If we don't examine carefully a passage of Scripture in matters of context, culture, and the meaning of key words, we risk misunderstanding the text. Not only will we miss out on what the text is saying, but we might even come up with something false and misleading. As I often tell my students, "To invent heresy or create a cult, all you need is a Bible and no context." Every cult is based on the Bible wrongly understood. Sound biblical interpretation is extremely important.[5]

Perhaps you agree that the Bible is important and that interpreting it correctly is important. But can we trust the manuscripts on which the Bible is based? You might be asking, "How do we know that the Bible has been transmitted accurately over the years? Have mistakes been made? Have people changed the text of the Bible?"

Reliability of the Ancient Manuscripts

In recent years some skeptics have asserted that the old manuscripts on which our modern Bible translations are based are riddled with errors and are completely unreliable.[6] According to these skeptics we don't know what the original writers of the books in the Bible actually wrote.

This skepticism is as unwarranted as it is extreme. Let me explain. Prior to the discovery of the Dead Sea Scrolls[7] (in the 1940s and 1950s), our oldest complete copy of the Old Testament (known as the Leningrad Codex) dated to about AD 1000. Another extensive but incomplete copy of the Old Testament dates to about AD 950. Apart from a few small fragments here and there, this was all we had to go on.

If our oldest complete copy of the Hebrew text of the Old Testament dates no earlier than AD 1000, then there is a gap of fifteen hundred years or more between the original writings and our oldest manuscript copies. Pointing this out, some skeptics suggested that the text of Scripture had probably been altered so that the text in AD 1000 is much different from what the original author wrote long ago.

This skepticism, however, has fallen on hard times. Thanks to the Dead Sea Scrolls, we now have portions (in some cases almost the entire text) of thirty-eight of the thirty-nine books of the Old Testament (Esther is the only missing book). In these scrolls we find that the *text is the same* as the text in the much later manuscripts that Bible translators for centuries relied upon. In other words, the text in the Bibles that you and I have today is *the same* as the text people were reading two thousand years ago. This came as quite a surprise to the skeptics.

The Dead Sea Scrolls take us a thousand years closer to the originals——that is, from AD 1000 back to the time of Jesus and even earlier. Let's consider the book of Isaiah for example. Isaiah finished writing his book of prophecy around 700 BC. Prior to the discovery of the Dead Sea Scrolls, there was a seventeen-century gap between Isaiah's original writing (700 BC) and our oldest copy of his book (AD 1000). Now, thanks to the discovery of the Great Isaiah Scroll from Cave 1, which dates to about 200 BC, we have gone back in time about twelve centuries. We are no longer seventeen centuries removed from the writing of Isaiah the prophet; we are only five centuries removed. Yet the text of Isaiah is the same. I suspect if we moved even further back in time thanks to more discoveries, the text would still be the same. The burden of proof now rests heavily on skeptics who claim without any evidence that the text of the Bible has been changed.

> The Dead Sea Scrolls take us a thousand years closer to the originals.

Some might object by saying that five centuries is a big gap. "Changes probably took place during this period of time," they suspect. Why should we assume that? If no changes took place over twelve hundred years, from 200 BC to 1000 AD, then why should we assume that changes took place between the original writing and 200 BC? Besides, historians often work with manuscripts that date anywhere from five hundred to one thousand years after they were composed. Examples include the work of Greek historians such as Thucydides and Herodotus and important Roman writers and historians such as Julius Caesar and Tacitus. Today's historians use copies of these Greek and Roman writings that date hundreds of years after the ancient authors wrote them, yet they reasonably assume that these manuscripts, which are relatively few in number, are reliable.

True, some of the scribes who made copies of biblical manuscripts did make mistakes. All books in antiquity were written by hand, letter by letter and word by word. The printing press wasn't invented until the fifteenth century. All scribes made mistakes when they copied books, whether secular or religious (and most errors were caught and corrected when the manuscript was proofread). Because we have thousands of manuscripts of the Bible, we therefore have thousands of copyist errors. But most of these errors are either corrected in the manuscripts (by the copyist himself or by a later corrector) or are easily identified because we have many other manuscripts that do not have the same errors. Through careful comparison of manuscripts scholars can identify the mistakes and determine the correct readings.

Let me say more about the New Testament manuscripts. We have today access to approximately fifty-eight hundred Greek manuscripts of the New Testament that predate the printing press. Of these, about fifty date before the year AD 300, a few date to the second century, and one—a small fragment of the Gospel of Mark—might even date to the first century. Compared to the manuscripts of classical Greece and Rome, the New Testament evidence is substantial. Not only do we have old Greek manuscripts, but we also have many old translations of the New Testament. We have at least ten thousand Latin manuscripts and another five thousand manuscripts in other languages. The New Testament manuscripts are old, numerous, and reliable. There is no literature from antiquity that rivals this remarkable record of preservation. There is no justification for the skepticism expressed from time to time in popular media and sometimes by scholars who should know better.[8]

There is even more evidence that boosts our confidence in the accuracy and reliability of the biblical manuscripts, especially relating to the New Testament. Thanks to the large number of ancient manuscripts recovered from Egypt (a half million pages of text from

Oxyrhynchus alone), we have today a lot of information about how in late antiquity books were produced, copied, studied, and circulated. One of the most amazing things we have learned is how long books were in use before being discarded. Some fifty-three libraries from antiquity have been recovered more or less intact. Of these, six yielded important chronological information. We have learned that books in antiquity remained in use anywhere from one hundred fifty years to four hundred years. The evidence from the Dead Sea Scrolls is similar. Many Bible scrolls had been in use for at least two hundred years before the community center at Qumran, near the Dead Sea, was destroyed by the Romans in the first century AD. Some of our best-preserved Greek Christian Bibles, which date to the fourth and fifth centuries AD, were in use for four hundred to six hundred years before being retired. This remarkable longevity really should not surprise us, for books in antiquity were very expensive.

This intriguing evidence suggests that the original New Testament writings (which scholars call *autographs*) were in circulation for a long time, being read, studied, and copied before being discarded or destroyed. Even if we assume only the minimum longevity (one hundred fifty years), this means that many of the original New Testament books would still have been in circulation at the beginning of the third century. Indeed, writing at the end of the second century, Latin church father Tertullian claims that several of Paul's original letters were still available for inspection in the cities to which they had been sent. Manuscript evidence uncovered in the last century suggests that Tertullian knew what he was talking about.[9]

Significantly, this discovery confirms that we have in our

possession today several large chunks of the Greek New Testament that date to the beginning of the third century. This means that when these copies were made, *the original writings were still available for study, comparison, and copying.* This important observation gives us every reason to believe that the text of the Greek New Testament, on which our modern language translations are based, reflects the text of the original writings of the New Testament authors. There is no legitimate basis for the idea that the books of the New Testament we have today are different in any significant way from the originals.

Historical and Factual Truth

Some skeptics will agree with everything that I have said thus far. "Yes, maybe the manuscripts are quite good and the text is well preserved," they concede. "But is there evidence that the stories they tell are true?" That is a fair question—and one you may be asking as well. After all, even if we are confident that our New Testament text is the same as the original writings, how do we know if the stories are factual? How do we know that they are not based on lies and legends? Is there any evidence *outside the Bible* that confirms the truthfulness of these stories?

As a matter of fact, substantial evidence supports the truthfulness of the stories narrated in the New Testament Gospels and book of Acts. This evidence falls into two general categories.

First, the Gospels and Acts are full of material that agrees with other sources, such as the writings of first-century Jewish historian Josephus. The New Testament speaks about real people (e.g., Roman governors like Pontius Pilate and Felix and Jewish high priests like Caiaphas and Annas), real customs (e.g., Passover, purity, Sabbath), and real political parties (e.g., Pharisees and Sadducees). What Josephus says about these people, purposes, and traditions agrees with the Gospels and Acts.[10]

Second, the New Testament Gospels and Acts agree with the archaeological, geographical, and topographical realities of the land of Israel in the first century AD. This is what historians call *verisimilitude*, a Latin word that means "true to reality." This is why historians and archaeologists make extensive use of the Gospels and book of Acts. Again and again, archaeological discoveries cohere with and sometimes dramatically confirm the narratives of the New Testament. (See the examples in chapter 12.) This would not be the case if the narratives talked about fictional characters and fictional events.

Further evidence for the truthfulness of the New Testament Gospels is found in the internal consistency of the story. The Roman crucifixion of Jesus of Nazareth for claiming to be the king of the Jews is rightly regarded as a solid fact of history. We must then ask, "Why was Jesus crucified as a royal pretender?" Had he simply been a moral teacher, a teller of parables meant to encourage greater faith in God, he would not have been viewed as a threat. A better explanation is the one that the Gospels provide (and the rest of the New Testament writings presuppose): Jesus proclaimed the coming kingdom of God and claimed to be Israel's anointed King. He was not a mere spiritual teacher whose message was misunderstood.

Also, we must ask, "Why did large crowds follow Jesus?" Most historians agree that crowds followed Jesus not simply because he was a compelling teacher but because he healed people. Had Jesus simply been a teacher who attempted to heal but failed, why would anyone follow him around listening to his teaching? Crowds surrounded and pressed Jesus, hoping to touch him, because they knew he in fact could heal.[11] Jesus was so successful at healing that other healers began to invoke his name in their attempts to heal people (Mark 9:38–40). This is astonishing and, I believe, unprecedented in the history of Israel. Jesus was so good at healing that his critics, who would have gladly denied Jesus' ability to heal, had no recourse but to claim that Jesus was in league with the devil. They couldn't deny the healings; they could only attribute them to a dark source in their attempt to discredit Jesus.

A man who was known as a powerful healer, who drew large crowds, who spoke of the approaching kingdom of God, and who dared to criticize the rulers of his day was a man to be feared by those who did not want the status quo threatened. This portrait of Jesus from the New Testament Gospels makes good sense and matches the evidence found in other sources (such as the first-century Jewish historian Josephus) and in materials recovered through archaeological excavations.

Summing Up and Looking Ahead

The Bible is a small library of books. These books are arranged in two parts: the Old Testament and the New Testament. The first part was written by Israelites (or Jews) and the second part was written by followers of Jesus, most of whom were Jews also. This second part, the New Testament, regards the first part as authoritative and presupposes its story and teachings. In fact, without the Old Testament the New Testament could not be fully understood.

There is significant and substantial evidence that both the Hebrew Old Testament and the Greek New Testament have been well preserved down through the centuries. We have many old manuscripts, both in the original languages and in early translations, which make it possible for scholars to confirm the original text. From archaeology and from other ancient sources we can confirm much of the history recounted in the Bible, giving us good reason to believe that the Bible is not only well preserved but also reliable.

In the next chapter we will look more closely at the individual books that make up the Bible. We will in greater depth inquire into what the Bible really says.

Why Does This Matter to Me?

❋ The Bible may be a very old collection of writings, but many of its stories are confirmed by archaeology and historical sources. We have very old copies of the Bible, and careful study has shown that the text of the Bible has been well preserved. This matters because it gives us the assurance that the Scripture is reliable, accurate, and trustworthy.

❋ The Bible's teaching has dramatically shaped the West and other parts of the world. Though old, the message of the Bible continues to be a force for positive progress everywhere it is read and heard. Many things in your life and mine today have been shaped—and will continue to be shaped—by the foundation of the Bible.

❋ There is no other book like the Bible. The question of God is the ultimate question. The Bible is the ultimate source. Why would anyone not read it and not carefully consider its message?

2

What's the Bible Saying, Really?

HAVE YOU EVER HEARD someone quote from the Bible? You might be surprised to learn that, more often than not, when the Bible is quoted by news shows and popular media, it is quoted out of context or even misquoted. For example, have you ever heard someone say, "Money is the root of all evil"? Actually, it is "The love of money is the root of all evil" (1 Timothy 6:10). That makes a big difference. Or how about, "The Lord helps those who help themselves"? This is probably the most quoted verse that does not in fact appear in the Bible! People claim to know the Bible, but they often fail to appreciate how the part they are quoting fits into the larger passage. Others misquote the Bible because they don't take into account the genre of the particular writing that is being quoted.

"What's a genre?" you ask. *Genre* refers to the form or type of literature. It could be a riddle, a proverb, a parable, a fable, a poem, a narrative, a song, a command, a prophecy, an allegory, or whatever. The list goes on. Most genres are easy to recognize. If someone began by saying, "Once upon a time, a handsome prince . . ." you would immediately think of a fairy tale. You would not ask for further details about time and place. If someone began with the words,

"Today it was reported . . ." you would think of a news report about an actual event. In this case you might ask for further details. If you heard someone begin with something like, "A rabbi, a priest, and a Baptist preacher went into a bar . . ." you know you are about to hear a joke (and you might offer to tell one of your own!).

All of this applies to the Bible. The books that make up the Bible are examples of one genre or another. Knowing which genre you are reading and how it functions is very important for understanding what the Bible is really saying.

The Genres in the Old Testament

The Old Testament includes historical narratives, books of prophecy, wisdom books, a collection of psalms, and a couple of songs. In some of these books more than one genre is present. For example, in a narrative book, such as Genesis or Judges, we encounter a few proverbs, parables, and prophetic oracles. Yet the writings are still books of narrative.

> Knowing which genre you are reading and how it functions is very important for understanding what the Bible is really saying.

Perhaps the most complicated book with respect to genre is Genesis. As its name implies, it is a book about origins. Genesis is a narrative, relating historical events from the creation of the world and the first humans to the family of Jacob who settled in the land of Egypt. The genres of the stories in the first eleven chapters are difficult to determine. For example, consider the great Flood (Genesis 6–9) and the Tower of Babel (11:1–9). Are these historical narratives or parables? Should they be taken literally or metaphorically?

Apart from the question of what kind of narrative we have in the book of Genesis, we encounter poetic utterances (e.g., Adam's utterance regarding Eve in Genesis 2:23; God's curse on the serpent in 3:14–16; Lamech's strange boast and threat in 4:23–24). We encounter genealogies (5:6–28), dreams (20:3, 6; 37:5), and deathbed testaments and prophecies (49:1–27). It is no wonder that scholars find study of the book of Genesis quite challenging.

The history of Israel continues in several narrative books, beginning with the Exodus (the deliverance from slavery in Egypt), the giving of the Law at Mount Sinai, and the time the Hebrew people spent in the wilderness. The books of Exodus, Leviticus, Numbers, and Deuteronomy recount this history. These books contain the Law of Moses, including the famous Ten Commandments.

The narrative book of Joshua describes Israel's conquest and settlement of the Promised Land, the land of Canaan.[1] The book of Judges comes next. It narrates a difficult, chaotic period in Israel's history, as the young nation, hardly more than a loose confederation of tribes, struggled within itself and with its not-so-friendly neighbors. One of the most colorful judges during this period was Samson. Set in this period is the beautiful story in the book of Ruth, which informs readers of David's immediate ancestors. Some scholars regard Ruth as quite possibly the world's first novel.

The books of Samuel and Kings narrate the history of the kingdom of Israel, from its establishment under Saul, Israel's first king, to its expansion and greatness in the tenth century BC under David and his son Solomon, and to its eventual collapse in the sixth century BC at the hands of the Babylonians. Although these writings are historical in the broad sense of the word, they are highly selective and not always in strict chronological sequence. Readers nee' to remember that these ancient narratives do not give us history the way we moderns think history ought to be written.

The books of the Prophets appear next in the Old Testament. Almost all the prophetic oracles are presented as poetry. They are highly metaphorical, which makes interpretation difficult. In a prophecy, metaphor functions more or less like a code. The code's symbols were usually well known and readily understood by the prophet's contemporaries, but these symbols are not as well known to us today. Through hard work we usually can determine most of the meaning, but some things remain unclear. The other issue with prophecy is that little of it is predictive. Old Testament prophecy is not so much concerned with foretelling as it is with forthtelling. That is, the Old Testament prophets spoke to Israel in the present much more than they spoke of the future.

The Bible includes three Major Prophets (four, if we include Daniel). They are Isaiah, Jeremiah, and Ezekiel. The prophet Ezekiel describes God's departure from Jerusalem and then foretells the coming of a Shepherd who will care for God's people. Added to the prophecy of Jeremiah is a short book known as Lamentations, a work that expresses great sorrow over the destruction of Jerusalem. The greatest of the Major Prophets is Isaiah. He famously speaks of a child who will be born, a son who will be given (Isaiah 9:1–7), whose "name will be called 'Wonderful Counselor, Mighty God, Everlasting Father, Prince of Peace'" (9:6). Every Christmas Christians recite this great oracle. Isaiah also speaks of a Servant of the Lord who will suffer for his people (52:13–53:12). Every Easter Christians give thought to this famous passage. Of course, the Prince of Peace celebrated at Christmas and the Suffering Servant remembered at Easter are one and the same.

Christians usually regard the book of Daniel as the fourth Major Prophet, though in the Jewish Old Testament Daniel is included in the Writings. Daniel envisions "one like a son of man" coming with the clouds of heaven, who will stand before God and receive power and a kingdom (7:13). Christians believe this vision was fulfilled in Jesus, who often spoke of himself as "the son of man," who on earth exercised authority and proclaimed the kingdom of God.

The remainder of the Prophets are gathered under the heading "the Twelve" or "the Twelve Minor Prophets." They are "minor" only because the books are brief in comparison to the much longer prophets. The shortest is Obadiah, comprising only one chapter of twenty-one verses. But the messages of the Minor Prophets are powerful.

A miscellany of writings makes up the remainder of the Hebrew Bible. A number of these writings fall under the category of Wisdom literature. These include the book of Job, which ponders the great question of why God sometimes allows the righteous to suffer and the wicked to prosper. The book of Psalms is a collection of Israel's greatest hymns. Some are lament psalms, in which the writer complains to God on behalf of Israel or perhaps on his own behalf. Other psalms celebrate the enthronement of Israel's king. Still others praise God for his greatness, for the beauty of creation, for his kindness to Israel, or for the goodness of his Law.

Proverbs is a collection of wise sayings and maxims. The collection likely began in Solomon's court (compiling proverbs in the courts of rulers was fashionable in the ancient Near East) and then continued for generations, growing into the marvelous collection we have in the Bible. These proverbs are not especially deep or learned; they are not supposed to be. What English writer and poet

Samuel Johnson said long ago fits well the purpose of Proverbs: "Men more frequently require to be reminded than informed." And that is just what the Proverbs do: they remind us of what is wise and what is foolish.

Ecclesiastes (also known as Qohelet, the Preacher), another Wisdom writing, gives thoughtful consideration to the uncertainties and ups and downs of life, recognizing that there is a time and season for everything. The book of Ecclesiastes, attributed to David's son Solomon, finds futility in the usual things humans think will bring joy and provides us with a sober warning. In startling contrast is the Song of Songs, also attributed to Solomon. The famous work is a lavish love song, filled with grand metaphors. The perspective of the Song of Songs (sometimes called Song of Solomon) could hardly be more at variance with the cynical views expressed in Ecclesiastes.

There are also some highly theological narratives. These include the two books of Chronicles, which recount the history of the kingdom of Israel. The author of Chronicles wrote long after the exile (ca. 587–520 BC), carefully noting which of Israel's kings did right in the sight of God and which did evil. The books of Ezra and Nehemiah were also written after the exile. They focus on the rebuilding of Jerusalem and the temple.

The Old Testament is a large and complex collection of writings of several genres. To interpret the Old Testament accurately, we must recognize and understand these genres. This is every bit as true in the case of the writings that make up the New Testament.

The Genres in the New Testament

Most scholars today recognize the New Testament Gospels as examples of biography, at least as biography was written in late antiquity.

During the days of the New Testament, a biography related what was considered important about the principal figure, his major activities and his major teachings. The New Testament Gospels do this. But biography and history in late antiquity were selective and interpretive. Writers of biography and history were not interested in dry facts; they interpreted the significance of the deeds and sayings of the persons whose stories they told. We see this in the New Testament Gospels.[2]

The Gospel accounts are not play-by-play recordings of Jesus. They are selective accounts. Sometimes they abbreviate and summarize the teaching of Jesus. One Gospel writer arranges Jesus' teaching a certain way, while another arranges it differently. Although broadly chronological, the Gospels are not chronological in a strict sense. The Gospel writers place stories in different locations, sometimes combining disparate elements. This is why we notice differences when we place the Gospels side by side and compare them. The Gospel writers also have different purposes for writing and have different ways of telling the Jesus story.

Matthew desires to show that Jesus is truly Israel's Messiah, the son of David, who fulfills prophecy from his birth to his death and throughout his public life and teaching. Matthew wants his readers to know that Jesus fulfilled the Law of Moses; he did not break it, nor does he teach his followers to break it. Nowhere does Matthew make that more clear than in the Sermon on the Mount (Matthew 5–7). Matthew seems to have written his account of the life of Jesus with the Jewish synagogue in mind, to Jews who doubted the truth of Jesus' teaching and whether he truly is Israel's awaited Messiah.

Mark is more concerned to challenge the Roman Empire. According to Roman belief, the emperor was the "son of God" through whom good news for the world began. Mark's Gospel suggests otherwise: "The beginning of the good news about Jesus the Messiah, the Son of God" (1:1 NIV). Mark presents Jesus as a commanding figure who has the authority to heal people, forgive people, feed multitudes, walk on water, and drive away evil spirits. Even in his death, Jesus shouts and an awestruck Roman centurion confesses, "Truly this man was the Son of God!" (Mark 15:39).

Luke wrote not only a Gospel account, but he also wrote the Acts of the Apostles, a brief account of the first generation of the early Church. Luke wants to show that the good news of Jesus is good news for the whole world. What began as a Jewish story has become a story for all of humankind. Luke is especially keen to show who God's true people are and on what basis. His Gospel shows that wealth is no sure sign of election and blessing, but proper stewardship and generosity are. In his second volume, the book of Acts, Luke shows that Paul's apostleship was legitimate and consistent with the preaching of Jesus' original apostles. Luke dedicated his Gospel and the book of Acts to a man he addresses as "most excellent Theophilus" (Luke 1:3; see also Acts 1:1). This man may have been a Roman magistrate, perhaps as part of Paul's legal defense.

The Gospel of John is noticeably different from the other three Gospels, which collectively are known as the Synoptic ("seen together") Gospels. Unlike the Synoptic Gospels, which focus on events in Galilee in the north, John's Gospel is focused on Judea and Jerusalem in the south. John introduces readers to new characters, such as Nicodemus and Lazarus, the latter of whom Jesus raised from the dead. John begins his Gospel by describing Jesus as the Word that became flesh (1:14), a Word who existed with God from the very beginning (1:1). In this way John is comparing Jesus with

God's eternal wisdom, which created the universe and brought light and truth to humankind.

Most of the remainder of the New Testament writings are letters. Thirteen are attributed to Paul. Three of these letters were written to pastors (1 Timothy, 2 Timothy, and Titus), so they are called the Pastoral Letters. One letter is a personal note to a man named Philemon, whose runaway slave Onesimus encountered Paul in prison. While incarcerated, Paul wrote three other letters (Ephesians, Colossians, and Philippians), which are called the Prison Letters. The recipients of these letters, respectively, were believers in Ephesus and Colossae (in Asia Minor—today's Turkey) and in Philippi (in Macedonia, north of Greece).

Paul's most important theological letters are two he wrote to the Christians in Corinth, in Greece (1 and 2 Corinthians), one to several churches in the region of Galatia, a district in Asia Minor (Galatians), and one to the Christians in Rome (Romans). The book of Romans is considered one of the most important letters ever written. In it Paul clearly spells out his understanding of the gospel, the good news of Jesus the Messiah. He argues forcefully that all humans stand before God in need of his

> The book of Romans is considered one of the most important letters ever written.

grace and forgiveness and that this grace and forgiveness are made available in God's Son, Jesus, who suffered and died on behalf of all of us. Paul makes very clear that in Jesus, the Messiah, Jews and non-Jews are brought together.

The New Testament also includes a number of other writings that are usually referred to as the General Letters. These are very Jewish in their orientation. Some of them are addressed to the exiles in the Dispersion and the twelve tribes (James 1:1), language that recalls Israel's history of being scattered and the nation's hope of someday being gathered by the Messiah. These letters include the book of Hebrews, which is more of a treatise than a letter. In this writing the author exhorts Jewish believers to remain faithful, to follow the examples of their Old Testament ancestors and heroes. The author reminds his readers how Jesus has fulfilled the requirements of the Law, how his death provided the ultimate sacrifice that need never be repeated, and how Jesus as the Great High Priest now intercedes for his people.

The letter of James, probably written by the half brother of Jesus, exhorts his readers to fulfill the royal law taught by Jesus—that is, to love our neighbor as ourselves (James 2:8). The apostle Peter describes the people of God as a "chosen race, a royal priesthood" (1 Peter 2:9), recalling what God said at Mount Sinai long ago: "You shall be to me a kingdom of priests" (Exodus 19:6). Second Peter and Jude warn God's people of coming judgment, while the author of 1 John, the longest of the three letters of John, assures his readers that God is a God of love who forgives his people.

Probably the most challenging New Testament book to interpret is the book of Revelation (sometimes called the Apocalypse). It is fitting that Revelation is the last book of the Bible, for this book focuses on last things—that is, the things that God has planned for the world in the future.

What makes Revelation difficult to interpret are its many symbols and metaphors. Moreover, we are not sure of the setting and context of this writing, so it is difficult to know whether these symbols refer to things in the author's time or to future things. One thing is clear, however: the author of the book of Revelation, who had a vision of the risen and exalted Jesus, knows full well that the future of the human race is firmly in God's hands and that someday righteousness will triumph over evil.

Why is it important for us to know the genres of the books of the Bible? Knowing what kind of literature the books of the Bible are helps us know how to interpret them. Not all the books should be interpreted the same way. For example, we should interpret Paul's letters as letters and compare them to other letters from his period of time. Comparison with other documents of the same genre helps us follow the author's train of thought, alerts us to certain features that play important roles in the argument, and explains the use and meaning of key words and phrases.

The Contents of the Bible and the Question of Canon

As I mentioned earlier, there is some variation in the contents of the Old Testament among the major Christian churches. These variations have to do with what is regarded as authoritative, which in turn has to do with the canon.

Literature that is regarded as authoritative (or, sometimes, as genuine) is referred to as *canonical*. This word comes from the Greek word *kanon*, which means "rule" or "measuring stick." Canonical literature is that literature against which other literature and ideas must be measured. For example, the ancient Greeks established the canon of various authors and playwrights, distinguishing the authentic writings from the fakes. The authentic collection was regarded as that author's canon.

Christians did the same thing with their authoritative writings. All theology and all practice were to be measured against the canon of the Christian Bible. So deciding what ought to be included in the canon was very important. Here is an overview of the Hebrew Bible, or Old Testament:

The Old Testament *(according to the Hebrew version)*

Law of Moses (or Pentateuch)	*The Prophets*	*The Writings*
Genesis	Joshua	Psalms
Exodus	Judges	Job
Leviticus	1 Samuel	Proverbs
Numbers	2 Samuel	Ruth
Deuteronomy	1 Kings	Song of Songs
	2 Kings	Lamentations
	Isaiah	Esther
	Jeremiah	Daniel
	Ezekiel	Ezra
	Hosea	Nehemiah
	Joel	Chronicles
	Amos	
	Obadiah	
	Jonah	
	Micah	
	Nahum	
	Habakkuk	
	Zephaniah	
	Haggai	
	Zechariah	
	Malachi	

You will notice that this arrangement of Old Testament books is according to the Hebrew version. The Hebrew version of the Old Testament is the official version of Judaism, only in this setting it is called the "Hebrew Bible" or Tanak. *Tanak* is an acronym referring to the three parts of the Hebrew Bible: the Torah or Law (which gives us the "T"), the Nevi'im or Prophets (which gives us the "N"), and the Ketuvim or Writings (which gives us the "K"). Since TNK cannot be pronounced, the "a" vowel is added to each syllable, giving us the word *Tanak* (sometimes spelled Tanach).

Most Protestant (non-Catholic) Christian churches use the Hebrew Bible as their Old Testament. English translations such as the King James, Revised Standard Version, New American Standard Bible, New International Version, and many others depend on the Hebrew Bible.

The Greek Orthodox Church and the Russian Orthodox Church use the Greek translation of the Hebrew Bible as their Old Testament. This Greek version of the Old Testament is available in English translation.[3]

All Christian denominations and churches agree as to the contents of the New Testament. As mentioned, the New Testament contains four Gospels; one book of Acts that narrates the first generation of the Church; several letters, most written by Paul; and one book of Revelation (or the Apocalypse). In the list below I group Acts with the Gospels because it is in fact volume two of the Luke–Acts work and because, like the Gospels, the book of Acts is narrative. I also include the book of Hebrews in the "Letters" column because although it could be classified as a treatise, it has a letter-like ending. Here is an overview of the contents of the New Testament:

The New Testament

Narratives (The Gospels and Acts)	*Letters*	*Apocalypse*
Matthew	Romans	Revelation
Mark	1 Corinthians	
Luke	2 Corinthians	
John	Galatians	
Acts of the Apostles	Ephesians	
	Philippians	
	Colossians	
	1 Thessalonians	
	2 Thessalonians	
	1 Timothy	
	2 Timothy	
	Titus	
	Philemon	
	Hebrews	
	James	
	1 Peter	
	2 Peter	
	1 John	
	2 John	
	3 John	
	Jude	

Roman Catholics, Greek Orthodox, and other Eastern Christians have several other books in the Old Testament called the Apocrypha, so their book count is higher. In these longer Old Testament versions, some of the books of the Apocrypha are imbedded in other books. For example, the Additions to the Book of Esther are added to the book of Esther. The Letter of Jeremiah is sometimes added to Baruch, becoming Baruch's chapter 6. The Prayer of Azariah and the Song of the Three Young Men, Susanna, and Bel and the Dragon are all added to the book of Daniel.[4]

The books of the Old Testament Apocrypha are as follows:

Books of the Old Testament Apocrypha

1 Esdras (the name and number vary in other versions)
2 Esdras (the name and number vary in other versions)
Tobit
Judith
Additions to the Book of Esther
Wisdom of Solomon
Ecclesiasticus (or Wisdom of Ben Sira)
Baruch
Letter of Jeremiah
Prayer of Azariah and Song of the Three Young Men
Susanna
Bel and the Dragon
Prayer of Manasseh
1 Maccabees
2 Maccabees
3 Maccabees
4 Maccabees
Psalm 151

Protestants sometimes react very negatively to the books of the Apocrypha, which is unfortunate. Some of these books served the early Church well, and a number of them appear in our oldest and most important ancient copies of Scripture. It was only during the Protestant Reformation that these books became a bone of contention, with some Protestants (especially the Puritans) insisting they be omitted from the Bible. In response to this position, the Roman Catholic Church, at the Council of Trent in 1546, officially canonized most of the books of the Apocrypha, dubbing them the "deuterocanonical" books (or "second canon"). You might be surprised to learn that the first printed editions of the King James Bible contained most of the books of the Apocrypha. Under Puritan pressure King James Bibles began to be printed without the Apocrypha, even though in some cases the names of these books still appeared in the table of contents!

The Apocrypha is useful for filling out our knowledge about events in Israel during the intertestamental period (the time between the Old and New Testaments). The books of the Maccabees are especially useful in this regard. Other books, like the Wisdom of Solomon and Ecclesiasticus (or Wisdom of Yeshua ben Sira), help us understand Jewish religious life and interpretation of Scripture in the generations immediately leading up to the time of Jesus.

There are some additional books that seem to have been popular in some Jewish and early Christian circles. One of these books is the *Book of Enoch* (also called *1 Enoch*). The men of Qumran (where the Dead Sea Scrolls were found) had at least twenty full or partial copies of it. Early Christians seemed to have liked it also, for the book of Jude in the New Testament quotes it. Another book that was a favorite at Qumran was *Jubilees*. The evidence suggests that, at least among some Jews in the first century BC and the first century AD, the books of *Enoch* and *Jubilees* may well have been thought of as authoritative Scripture. Today the *Book of Enoch* has semicanonical status in the Ethiopian Church.

Who decided what to include in the canon? In Dan Brown's wildly inaccurate *The Da Vinci Code*, the fictional character Sir Leigh Teabing (an anagram for Richard *Leigh* and Michael *Baigent*, popular writers whose misleading books inspired the naive Dan Brown) claims that Emperor Constantine chose the books of the Bible. This of course is not true. Almost everything Sir Leigh asserts in Brown's inexplicably popular novel is false.

Although the canon of Scripture was formally recognized in a series of councils in the fourth century and later (well after the death of Constantine), the authority of the first-century writings was recognized before the ink dried on the papyrus. These early writings were recognized by the individuals, groups, and churches to which they had been sent. Thus the process of canonization was both immediate and gradual. The only formal councils in the first century, narrated in Acts 11 and 15, had to do with important theological questions (centered on whether non-Jews could become Christians and, if so, which Jewish traditions, if any, must they observe). In these councils the apostles presided, and no one challenged their authority. We should assume the apostles had the same authority with regard to their writings.

Summing Up and Looking Ahead

In this chapter we looked at the message of the Bible, asking what the Bible really says. We again considered the importance of genres, looking at examples ranging from Genesis and Isaiah to the Psalms and Wisdom writings in the Old Testament, and from the Gospels and Acts to the Letters and Revelation in the New Testament. We also considered the contents or "canon" of the two Testaments, exploring the rationale for including some books and excluding others. We found that the process of recognizing books as authoritative (and therefore *canonical*) was an informal and gradual one that in later church councils received more formal recognition. Some of the things briefly discussed in chapters 1 and 2 will be pursued in greater detail in later chapters.

What Is in This Book and How It Unfolds

Before bringing part 1 to a close, allow me to provide you with a road map so you will have a better sense of where the rest of the book is going. Eleven chapters follow. You will find chapters 3 through 9 in part 2. The focus of this part of the book is on what the Bible is all about. Chapter 3 asks why a story about creation is important. This chapter will show you what the Bible says about the beginning of the cosmos and the beginnings of the human story. You will be introduced to the patriarchs and matriarchs (our first fathers and mothers) and how God worked in their lives.

Chapter 4 confronts the apparent negativity and legalism in the Old Testament. Why all the rules and negative talk? You may think all of this is obsolete and outmoded. Time to move on. Or is it? We need to take a fresh look at some of this very old stuff. You will be surprised at how relevant and meaningful it remains.

In chapter 5 we will look at the bright side of the Old Testament, its many promises and assurances. We will find that these promises are just as relevant and life enriching as they were when they were first spoken long ago. Chapter 6 looks at what happens when the truths of the Bible are ignored. In this chapter we see the ups and downs of the people of Israel and their rulers. You will see that God's grace is still very much at work even when people make terrible decisions.

In chapter 7 we move into the New Testament and into the world and life of Jesus. Where did Jesus come from? What did he teach and what did he do? You have probably heard that Jesus proclaimed the kingdom of God. But what did that mean to the people of his time? What does it mean to us? You will be surprised at the answers to these questions.

Chapter 8 asks about the relevance of Jesus for us today. After all, he may have been important long ago; he may even have changed the world. But is he still significant in our time? Does it really matter if people hear about Jesus anymore?

In chapter 9 we look at one of the most controversial themes relating to the Bible: how it ends. What does the Bible say about our future? No topic has been more sensationalized and misrepresented. You will be surprised by what the Bible has to say about humanity's destiny.

In the third and final part of this book, chapters 10 through 14, I will address a number of important questions. Chapter 10 asks how we can know what the Bible means. You will learn how you can interpret the Bible, step by step, accurately and fairly. It's work, but it's not rocket science!

In chapter 11 we will look at passages in the Bible that express anger and violence. The Bible contains a lot of history, and in some of this history is some pretty nasty stuff. How do we understand it? Given the Islamic violence in the world, in which horrible things are done in the name of God, how are we to understand the Bible's stories of violence? Related to this is the question that asks if the New Testament is anti-Jewish or anti-Semitic. This, too, is a sensitive question that deserves a careful answer.

Chapter 12 surveys important archaeological discoveries relating to the Bible. I think you will find this discussion very interesting. A lot of people have no idea how many discoveries confirm the people and events in the Bible. There is a surprising amount of archaeological evidence that supports the truthfulness of biblical narratives.

Chapter 13 sums up who did what and when it happened. It is important to have a sense of sequence. The order of events functions as a skeleton, as it were, on which historians hang the meat of their narrative. We need to know which bone is connected to which bone.

Why Does This Matter to Me?

* Knowing what kind of literature (or genre) is in the Bible helps us interpret and apply it much more accurately. Given the importance of the Bible, why would we settle for less?
* Rightly interpreting the Bible means that we can avoid misunderstanding and misapplying its message.
* Rightly understood, the Bible is rich with relevant meaning. That means you and I can get out of it what was all along meant for us to get out of it. This is great news!

Part Two

WHAT IS THE BIBLE ABOUT?

3

Why Do We Need
a Creation Story?

HAVE YOU EVER WONDERED, *Is there really a God?* It's hard to think of a more important question.

Throughout history most people have believed in God (or gods). Indeed, polytheism (belief in many gods) at one time was the norm, and it is still popular in countries like India. Most people today who believe in God (such as Jews, Christians, Muslims, Sikhs, and others) are monotheists—that is, they believe in *one* God. Monotheists do not necessarily believe the same things about God, but most agree that God is powerful, loving, and wise. However, this widely held belief is today rejected by many, including a number of celebrities and media personalities.

So the question remains: does God exist? To speak intelligently about the existence of God, we need to know the whole story. The creation of the universe is a big part of that story, which is why the Bible tells us about creation. Without the story of creation we would not have the context necessary to understand good and evil in the world.

> To speak intelligently about the existence of God, we need to know the whole story.

Perhaps you have heard someone ask (or have asked someone), "If God is powerful and loving, then why is there evil in the world? Why do tragedies occur? Why do innocent children die?" To some skeptics the reality of evil in our world suggests either that God is not powerful and so cannot prevent evil, or that God is powerful but evidently does not love us because he allows evil. He seems indifferent to our suffering. "If God is there, then he doesn't care," I heard one agnostic say. The "problem of evil," as it usually is called, has destroyed or prevented faith for many people. Some believe that the Bible does not provide an answer for this important question.[1]

The Bible does in fact address the problem of evil. It explains why there is evil, injustice, suffering, and tragedy in the world. The Bible also explains what I call the "problem of good"—that is, why there are so many good things in the world, why people do generous things, love, appreciate and wish to create beauty, care for the sick and needy, and sometimes even give their lives for others. In short, the Bible explains why humans innately recognize right and wrong and why they know these things are important.

The Bible gives us the big picture of where we came from and why we are here. It places us in the context of space and time, and in the context of purpose and meaning. The Bible does not take the place of science, nor is it antagonistic toward science.[2] The Bible explains the whys and wherefores, the things science cannot explain. The Bible addresses the ultimate questions. The first question concerns origins: Where did we come from?

Creation

The Bible begins with the beginning itself: "In the beginning God created the heavens and the earth" (Genesis 1:1 NIV). Modern science at one time rejected the idea of a beginning, holding instead to the view that the universe was eternal.[3] In the 1950s and 1960s, however, scientists recognized that the universe did indeed have a beginning (popularly called the Big Bang) and that physical matter is not eternal. This discovery created a problem for atheists because scientists know that *something* cannot come from *nothing*. Not surprisingly, a growing number of scientists now believe that some powerful and intelligent Being initiated or created the universe.[4]

Ongoing scientific research—thanks in large part to the Hubble Telescope—has shown how amazing our solar system is and how unique the planet Earth is. Not only is our planet perfectly suitable for complex life, but it is perfect in design and location to enable intelligent life to study the universe. The odds for all of this to have happened by chance are extremely slight, perhaps nonexistent.[5]

> The Bible does in fact address the problem of evil.

The creation story in Genesis is not scientific in any modern sense. This was never its intention. Its principal purpose is to reveal that the universe came about by a loving Creator God, who designed planet Earth in a way that not only sustains human life but maximizes our opportunities for cultural, intellectual, and spiritual growth. Ours is a world of remarkable beauty, abundance, diversity, and wonder.

Our world offers us far more than what we need to survive. It presents us with sights, sounds, tastes, and aromas that go way beyond the necessities. Our world instructs us, inspires us, fills us with awe, and points to the creative power of a loving God. It is no wonder the Hebrew psalmist long ago declared, "The heavens are telling the glory of God; and the firmament proclaims his handiwork. Day to day pours forth speech, and night to night declares knowledge" (Psalm 19:1–2). Creation does indeed proclaim the greatness and goodness of God.

The message of the creation story in Genesis becomes much clearer when we compare it to the creation stories in the ancient Near East. We have stories from Egypt, Sumer, Assyria, Babylon, and other ancient city-states and kingdoms. In all of them, typically after a series of battles, a hierarchy of gods emerges. For example, one Egyptian creation story goes like this:

> The All-Lord said, after he had come into being: "I am he who came into being as Khepri [the morning sun god]. When I had come into being, being (itself) came into being, and all beings came into being after I came into being. Many were the things which came forth from my mouth, before heaven came into being, before earth came into being, before the ground and creeping things had been created."[6]

This story goes on to tell of the defeat of a great dragon.

In the ancient Babylonian story called *Enuma Elish* ("When on High"), probably the best-known ancient creation story apart from Genesis, we read:

> When on high the heaven had not been named, firm ground below had not been called by name, naught but primordial Apsu [God of fresh water], their begetter, (and) Mummu-Tiamat ["mother"-goddess of salt-water], she who bore them all, their waters commingling as a single

body; no reed hut had been matted, no marsh land had appeared, when no gods whatever had been brought into being.[7]

The story goes on to describe the battle between the parent gods (Apsu and Tiamat) and the younger gods, led by the heroic Marduk, who slays Tiamat and her commander Kingu. From the former he forms the sky and sea; from the latter's blood he creates people. As his reward Marduk is given lordship of the universe. If you are familiar with Greek mythology, this creation story will remind you of the defeat of the Titans at the hands of the younger Olympian gods, led by Zeus. In all of these stories the gods are themselves part of creation. There is no god who is apart from creation itself.

Although there are some parallels between the creation story of Genesis 1–2 and other ancient Near Eastern creation stories, the differences are noticeable and significant. First and foremost, Genesis speaks of only one God, through whom all of creation came into being. There are no squabbling deities and no mighty Titans to overthrow. Second, creation is distinct from God himself. The heavens and the earth are not made from the bodies of slain gods or somehow accidentally left over from battles and destruction. Third, according to Genesis, God created the heavens and earth in an orderly and systematic way. With respect to each stage of creation God sees that "it was good" (1:4, 10, 12, 18, 21, 25). Each stage was designed. The Genesis creation story concludes with the words: "And God saw everything that he had made, and behold, it was very good" (1:31). Finally, human beings are created in the image of God (1:26). Humans hold no special place in the creation

53

stories of the ancient Near East, but they do in the creation story in the book of Genesis.

The differences between the creation story in Genesis and other creation stories of the ancient Near East could not be starker.[8] In contrast to these stories, Genesis declares that all of creation is good, all of it has a purpose, and the high point of creation is humanity, whom God blesses, gives the earth to care for, and commands to multiply (1:26–30). The creation story of Genesis reveals a loving God who has prepared a healthy, beautiful, and enduring home for the beings he has made in his own image.

This is one of the most important teachings in the Bible. It means that you and I are very important. We are much, much more than intelligent, two-legged animals. Our very existence is part of God's design and plan. We are so important to God that he has taken the trouble to provide for us in a way that we might not only survive but flourish. All of this implies that our lives have meaning and purpose.

Thanks to modern science we can now appreciate how well made, protective, and nurturing our planet is. Our planet is warmed by a sun that is just the right size, a sun that emits higher than average photonic energy but lower than average levels of dangerous radiation.[9] This means that our sun has what it takes to support life but at the same time not destroy it. Our planet and the other planets in our solar system have stable orbits. (Irregular orbits, like the erratic orbits of planets in other solar systems, would pose great danger to life on planet Earth.) Our planet is protected by several large gaseous planets (Jupiter, Saturn, Uranus, and Neptune) that shield us from catastrophic impacts by asteroids. Our planet has an optimal rotation, an ideal tilt of its axis, and an orbiting moon that is just the right distance from the Earth, travels at an optimal speed, energizes our tides, and stabilizes the Earth's rotation. It is this fine-tuning of our world that weighs so heavily against atheistic theories of random chance.[10]

There is even more fine-tuning to be considered. The planet Earth has a liquid, molten center that permits continental drift and tectonic plate movement. Without this feature we would have no mountains. In fact, most if not all of the land on our planet would be under water if it were not for the movements of land-masses. Our planet's core is highly metallic, which creates our magnetic poles, which stabilize our atmosphere and together with our atmosphere protect us from deadly radiation from outer space and our own sun. In addition, our planet has enormous quantities of water, without which complex life would not be possible.

These are only some of the most important features of our life-sustaining planet. There are many more. All of these amazing features underscore the words spoken long ago: "And God saw everything that he had made, and behold, it was very good" (Genesis 1:31).

The human being is the high point of God's creation. There is nothing like us. We may be made of essentially the same stuff from which many animals are made, but in all the important ways we are vastly different. Scientists sometimes point out that apes and chimpanzees are very close to humans, with a DNA overlap of approximately 96 percent.[11] True enough, but the 4 percent makes all the difference in the world. Brains of apes and chimpanzees do not possess the capacity for language and abstract thought.[12] No ape wonders what life is all about. No chimpanzee asks where he came from and what the future holds. In short, apes and chimpanzees do not ask the big questions. They do not even know that there are questions to ask.

Humans are distinctive, too, in their appreciation of beauty. Only humans are aware of the beauty of sight and sound and then in a variety of ways attempt to imitate, interpret, and expand upon it. No ape has ever composed a symphony or endeavored to paint a portrait. No ape has grappled with moral issues or pondered what is right and wrong. But humans do all these things. Humans are aware of the wonder of the world. Humans are moral and spiritual beings. Humans rejoice in what is good but are troubled by evil. Humans wonder where God is in all of this. No animal gives a moment's thought to any of these things.

The psalmist was so impressed with wonder of human life that he declared to God:

I praise you, for I am fearfully and wonderfully made.
Wonderful are your works;
    my soul knows it very well.
My frame was not hidden from you,
when I was being made in secret,
    intricately woven in the depths of the earth.
Your eyes saw my unformed substance;
in your book were written, every one of them,
    the days that were formed for me,
    when as yet there was none of them. (Psalm 139:14–16)

The language of this passage strikes us moderns as quaint. Though it is not scientific, it contains great truth. We humans are indeed wonderfully made. There is nothing in the physical world that comes close to the human brain. Recent discoveries in neuroscience are breathtaking. How our brains think, make decisions, create, and access memory is astounding. Ongoing research is also probing the spiritual and moral dimension of humans. Intriguingly, studies show that the human being is much more than a mere physical brain.[13] These studies seriously undermine the theories of atheists and materialists who reject the existence of God and the reality of the spiritual or nonmaterial.[14] In fact, the findings of modern science convinced longtime philosopher and atheist Antony Flew that there must be a God after all.[15]

The complex functions of human language, thought, and memory are astounding. Not even the most powerful computer can compare, for computers are nothing more than data storage and retrieval mechanisms whose functions are programmed *by humans*. Computers cannot think or make independent decisions, no matter what you see on television or read in popular science fiction.[16]

Thanks to the Human Genome Project we now know that human DNA contains more than three billion bits of information, that almost all human cells contain this information, and that each human being has anywhere from ten trillion to one hundred trillion cells. These facts boggle the mind. No wonder the psalmist expressed his amazement.

Throughout most of its work Dr. Francis Collins headed up the Human Genome Project. Perhaps the single most astonishing discovery was that the human genome is a code. And *code* is another word for *language*. The implications of this discovery are enormous, for mindless chance speaks no language. Dr. Collins rightly concluded that the human genome sequence, which he calls "the language of God," provides clear evidence of an intelligent, creative power.[17]

What Genesis says about creation, and specifically about human beings, is supported by modern science and, I am sure, will receive additional support in future research and discovery. But the book of Genesis has more to say about creation and our responsibilities as human beings.

Obligations

In the creation account in Genesis, God gave humans dominion over all the earth (1:26–30). This has sometimes been understood that the earth is ours to do with as we please. Such thinking has led to shortsighted exploitation of resources, waste, pollution, and extinction of many species. This is not what the Bible teaches. Genesis says that humans are made in God's image; we are the rulers of the earth and as such are responsible to protect and care for the earth, as surely as it is required of a king to protect his realm. Humanity rules over animals, but animals are humanity's companions (Genesis 2:18–20) and are to be treated humanely (Exodus 23:19; Proverbs 12:10). The Psalmist reminds us, "the earth is the LORD's and the fullness thereof" (Psalm 24:1). The earth does not belong to humans; it belongs to God.

Because the earth is the Lord's we are obligated to care for it. We do this out of respect for God, out of appreciation for the earth itself, and out of our interests too. After all, the earth is our home. It only makes sense to take good care of it.

And because humans are created in God's image, we too, in a sense, can further develop the created order. We can imitate the art we see in nature. We can develop the technologies we see at work in nature. We can graft plants and cross-pollinate to create new species and new varieties. We create gardens, plant groves of trees, restock streams and lakes, and do many things that preserve and enhance our world.

We have seen that creation tells us many important things about the Creator. Genesis declares that humans have been made in the image of God (1:26). This means, among other things, that we can think about things and make decisions. Humans have free will. We may choose to do right or to do wrong. We have the freedom to seek God and his ways or to ignore him and go our own way. Unfortunately, this freedom has resulted in a lot of problems—problems we should not blame on God.

Speaking of problems, let's take a look at what Genesis tells us about our ancestors. We usually regard these notable ancients as heroes, but when we read the stories carefully, we find that most of them are people very much like us.

Ancestors

The first eleven chapters of Genesis underscore the positive creative power of God, who fashioned a good heaven and earth on the one hand, and humankind, some of whom chose the rebellious, foolish nature on the other. Scholars debate how to interpret these early stories and in what sense they represent historical persons and events.[18] But most agree that the message is clear: Humans have a tendency to estrange themselves from God and from one another. This is why we now live in a fallen world, a world marked by strife and evil. Nevertheless, God remains active in his world, wooing humanity back to himself. This story centers on our ancestors—a man named Abraham and his descendants.

Abraham

In the midst of the idolatry, polytheism, and immorality of the people in Chaldea (in the Middle Eastern region known as Mesopotamia—today's Iraq) God called a man to himself:

> The Lord said to Abram, "Go from your country and your kindred and your father's house to the land that I will show you. And I will make of you a great nation, and I will bless you, and make your name great, so that you will be a blessing. I will bless those who bless you." (Genesis 12:1–3)

This remarkable promise is repeated several times in Genesis (15:1–5; 17:1–8; 22:15–18). In essence God promised Abram three things: land, posterity, and blessing.

Abram, whose name becomes Abraham ("the father of a multitude"), and his wife, Sarai, whose name becomes Sarah ("princess"), become the fountainhead from which the nation of Israel will spring. In the Bible—and in later literature—Abraham and Sarah become models of virtue, serving as the benchmark for fidelity and righteousness in Jewish, Christian, and Islamic traditions. Yet this celebrated couple was far from perfect.

One thing that impresses me about the stories of the patriarchs and matriarchs is that the Bible tells it like it is. Nobody's story gets whitewashed. And that goes for Abraham and Sarah. For all of their fidelity to God, they suffer lapses from time to time. Twice Abraham, fearing his life is in danger, lies about his wife, claiming she is his sister (Genesis 12:10–20; 20:1–18). He also expresses doubt that God will give him a son in his old age as promised (15:4; 17:16, 19; 18:10). Sarah not only doubts this wondrous promise but laughs at the idea—and then denies that she did so (18:10–15). When she finally does give birth to a son, Sarah names him Isaac, which in Hebrew means "laughter" (21:6). This name recalls Sarah's own laughter when she first heard God's promise. She laughed (in derision) when the promise was given; she laughed again (in joy) when the promise was fulfilled.

Of the three things God promised Abraham (land, posterity, and blessing), only one—posterity—was fulfilled in Abraham's lifetime. Even that fulfillment, however, seemed doubtful. After all, a single son in an era when families were large and survival rates uncertain hardly guaranteed the eventual emergence of a "great nation" or multitude of descendants. Moreover, this partial fulfillment was placed in danger when God asked Abraham to offer up Isaac as a sacrifice (Genesis 22). Here Abraham's faith in God was put to the supreme test, and this time Abraham did not waver. He did as he was told, and as he raised the knife God intervened: "Do not lay your hand on the boy or do anything to him, for now I know that you fear God, seeing you have not withheld your son, your only son, from me" (v. 12).[19] Two millennia later God himself did not withhold his only Son, through whom the promise of blessing was fulfilled.

> The Bible tells it like it is. Nobody's story gets whitewashed.

Jacob

Perhaps the most colorful of the patriarchs was Jacob, Abraham's grandson. Jacob, whose name means "one who supplants," was a rascal in his youth. He lived up to his name by cheating his older brother, Esau, out of his birthright (Genesis 25:27–34). To do this he deceived his father, Isaac (27:5–45). Jacob was himself cheated by his uncle Laban (29:13–30). He later returned the favor (30:25–31:55).

After separating from his uncle on poor terms Jacob encountered his brother, Esau (Genesis 32–33). Fearing revenge, Jacob divided his family and servants into two camps, so that if one camp were attacked, the other would escape. During this time of fear and uncertainty Jacob encountered a mysterious man in the wilderness (32:22–32). He wrestled with this person until daybreak. Although his hip was injured, Jacob would not give up and let go without a blessing from the stranger. Jacob got his blessing and more: "Your name shall no longer be called Jacob, but Israel, for you have striven with God and with men, and have prevailed" (32:28). The stranger never explicitly identifies himself, but Jacob and all readers of this story suspect that the stranger was none other than God himself, for it was God who changed the names of Abraham and Sarah. Now God has changed Jacob's name. Greatly moved by his experience Jacob called the place of his encounter Peniel ("Face of God"), acknowledging that he had seen God face to face yet still lived (32:30).

Jacob—now renamed Israel ("he who strives with God")—is now ready to meet his brother, Esau. No longer running, no longer hiding, Jacob approached Esau and bowed before him (Genesis 33:3). Then something unexpected happened: "Esau ran to meet him and embraced him, and fell on his neck and kissed him, and they wept" (33:4). Esau has forgiven Jacob. The once estranged brothers greet one another, exchange gifts and kind words, and part on good terms. The narrative suggests that things changed for Jacob after his encounter with the stranger. That is undoubtedly true. But the generosity and forgiveness exhibited by Esau are remarkable. Although cheated of his father's blessing, Esau extends to his selfish brother every courtesy and accommodation. No wonder this elder brother served as the template in a parable Jesus told many centuries later (the parable of the prodigal son; Luke 15:11–32).

At Bethel Jacob's change of name to Israel is confirmed and the covenant (a treaty or contract) originally made with Abraham is renewed (Genesis 35:10–12). God tells Israel, "I am God Almighty: be fruitful and multiply. A nation and a company of nations shall come from you, and kings shall come from your own body. The land that I gave to Abraham and Isaac I will give to you, and I will give the land to your offspring after you" (35:11–12).

Joseph and Judah

Jacob's troubles, however, are far from over. Motivated by revenge for the mistreatment of their sister Dinah, Jacob's sons murdered the men of Shechem and plundered their village (Genesis 34). Because of this violence Jacob and his family had to leave the region. But even greater grief overtook the patriarch, this time much closer to home. Seized by jealousy over the favoritism shown Joseph (Jacob's younger son) and vexed by his dreams foreshadowing his own greatness, Jacob's older sons plotted the murder of their younger brother Joseph (Genesis 37). Although in the end they did not kill Joseph but sold him into slavery, they cruelly deceived their father Jacob by allowing him to believe that Joseph had been killed by a wild animal. Jacob was inconsolable: "I shall go down to Sheol to my son, mourning" (37:35).[20]

This treachery sets the stage for a remarkable contrast between the fidelity of Joseph and the faithlessness of his older brothers. A graphic illustration of this contrast takes place in Genesis 38–39. Joseph's brother Judah had three sons, the eldest of whom married a woman named Tamar. The elder son died before Tamar conceived a child, so in keeping with the ancient custom of levirate marriage, Tamar was given to Judah's second eldest son.[21] The second son, however, did not want Tamar to become pregnant. He probably wanted Tamar to remain childless so that he might gain a greater portion of his father's property. In any case, his refusal to impregnate her brings about his own death. The consecutive deaths of his sons frightened Judah, so he puts off Tamar, asking her to remain a widow in her father's house while the younger, third son grows to maturity. Judah probably had no intention to marry his third son to Tamar, custom or no custom.

Tamar recognized that her prospects were not good. She faced the possibility of going through life without a husband or children. This was a terrible misfortune in the ancient Near East, where widowed, childless women were vulnerable to abuse, neglect, even starvation. In her desperation Tamar disguised herself as a prostitute and deceived her recently widowed father-in-law Judah. Months later Tamar was found to be pregnant. The family was horrified. Judah commanded, "Bring her out and let her be burned!" (Genesis 38:24). When to his surprise and great embarrassment Judah discovered that he was the father of the expected child, he confessed publicly, "She is more righteous than I" (38:26).

In great contrast to sinful and hypocritical Judah is Joseph, who was falsely accused and wrongfully imprisoned (Genesis 39–40). If anyone had grounds for abandoning his faith in God, it was Joseph, who was betrayed by his jealous brothers, sold into slavery, sent away to a foreign land, tempted by another man's wife, slandered, and thrown into prison. Yet through it all Joseph remained faithful, trusting that in all of his troubles God was still with him.

I have described some of the follies of these patriarchs in order to make the point that what we are reading in Genesis are not idealized, varnished accounts of saintly persons. The Bible tells it like it was and like it is. What we read in the Bible are stories of real human beings, people who find faith, experience God, and through this experience are transformed. In many ways the lives of our ancient ancestors were not too different from our own. Can we not all identify with these patriarchs and matriarchs at certain points? If God can make good things happen despite their failings, can he not do the same with us?

> The lives of our ancient ancestors were not too different from our own.

The Bible's candor is why we believe that the patriarchs were real people, people of history, and not fictional characters. Writers of fiction would have exaggerated the virtues of Israel's ancestors and would have missed no opportunity to vilify Israel's enemies. But this is not what we see in the Bible stories. The shortcomings of the patriarchs are acknowledged, along with the righteousness and generosity of their rivals, sometimes even their enemies. This is not the stuff of pious fiction. It is what we should expect in narratives that truthfully relate the lives of real people.[22]

The book of Genesis ends on several positive notes. The aged patriarch Jacob and his extended family are reunited with Joseph, who provides for them in Egypt. On his deathbed Jacob blesses his sons. Some of these blessings, which include several promises and prophecies, anticipate important things to come, which will be considered in the next chapter.

Summing Up and Looking Ahead

The Bible's book of Genesis provides us with the only story of creation from antiquity that speaks of one God—not many—a God who with great power and wisdom created a world ideally suited for human beings, creatures made in his own image. Because humans are made in the image of God they can think and make choices of their own free will. This freedom explains a great deal about the condition in which humanity finds itself today.

The problems we face today have their roots in antiquity. Even the celebrated patriarchs and matriarchs revered by Jews, Christians, and Muslims were far from perfect, often sinning and failing in ways that very much remind us of ourselves.

But none of this took God by surprise. He knew our natures and proclivities all too well. This is why God gave us laws and moral principles by which we are protected from one another and by which we may flourish. Along with the laws he also made us several promises.

Why Does This Matter to Me?

- ❀ The old stories of Genesis tell us a lot about ourselves— our fears, foibles, and failings—and a lot about God. One of the comforting things these old stories tell us is that God is forgiving and fully able and inclined to put back together the broken pieces—if we let him.
- ❀ The Bible reveals that God was "green" long before going green became fashionable. God made a beautiful, healthy world, and he wants us to keep it that way. We are to develop the world but not destroy it.

❀ God made the world in such a way that it instructs us. When we study creation, we learn about the universe and can explore and discover the greatness of God's creative power.

4

Isn't the Bible Just Rules and Negative Talk?

THE BEAUTIFUL WORLD God fashioned is more than sufficient to sustain and nurture us. The planet Earth is ours to enjoy, explore, study, cultivate, and admire. Why should we expect anything more of God? Has he not already given us more than enough?

Some people, with only a vague or distorted knowledge of the Bible, might say that God has given us too much—too many rules, that is. A lot of people have the impression that the Bible is a book of rules and negative talk. Who needs that anymore? Well, as we shall see, there is a lot more to it. Yes, there are some rules—and there are some promises.

Running throughout the Bible is the message that God loves us and gently draws us to himself. To be complete as human beings, who are made in God's image (Genesis 1:26), we need God, to know of him, to know him, and to be guided by him. We do not need more earth, more water, more air, or more sunshine. We need more of God. In the words of the great fifth-century Christian thinker Augustine: "You have formed us for yourself, and our hearts are restless until they find rest in you."[1] To answer the ultimate questions in life we must learn from God, what he has revealed in the universe and what he has revealed in human history.

Our need for God is never seen more clearly than when we turn our back on God. Ignoring God leads invariably to idolatry of one form or another and to a host of moral and spiritual problems. In the last half-century or so the West has moved away from God, embracing paganism, materialism, and immorality to a degree that our grandparents would not have believed possible. Ours is a generation of self-indulgence, narcissism, hedonism, materialism, vulgarity, and easy morals. It was in a setting not too different from what we are experiencing today that the story of Abraham began.

Promises

Jacob's Blessings

When God called Abraham out of the land of the Chaldeans he promised him land, posterity, and blessing. God repeated these promises to Abraham's son Isaac and to his grandson Jacob. These promises underlay the blessings Jacob pronounced on his sons, whose descendants became the tribes of Israel. All these blessings are prophetic in one sense. On his deathbed Jacob summoned his sons, saying, "Gather yourselves together, that I may tell you what shall happen to you in days to come" (Genesis 49:1).

One of the patriarch's blessings is especially interesting, for it hints at the coming Messiah (or Christ, meaning "anointed") and Savior, through whom God's original promises made to Abraham would be fulfilled. Jacob says to his son Judah:

Judah, your brothers shall praise you;
> your hand shall be on the neck of your enemies;
> your father's sons shall bow down before you.

Judah is a lion's cub;
> from the prey, my son, you have gone up.
He stooped down, he couched as a lion,
> and as a lioness; who dares rouse him up?
The scepter shall not depart from Judah,
> nor the ruler's staff from between his feet,
until tribute comes to him;
> and to him shall be the obedience of the peoples.
> (Genesis 49:8–10)

At the very least this blessing promises a royal dynasty. Judah's brothers will "bow down" before him—that is, their descendants will bow before the kings who will descend from Judah the patriarch. In the history of Israel this prophecy was fulfilled in the reign of David, who was from the tribe of Judah, and his many royal descendants. But does Jacob's blessing envision something more?

At least one century before the birth of Jesus, Judah's words in Genesis 49:8–12 came to be understood as a prophecy concerning the awaited Messiah. In the Aramaic translation of the Bible, which developed over time in the synagogue, the messianic and prophetic dimension of Judah's blessing is made clear. The words "the scepter shall not depart in Judah" in verse 10 become in the Aramaic translation "kings shall not cease from among those of the house of Judah." In the same verse the words "until he comes to whom it belongs" become in the Aramaic "until the time King Messiah shall come, to whom the kingship belongs." Although this Aramaic paraphrase comes from a later time, it makes explicit the interpretations we find in much earlier writings, such as the Dead Sea Scrolls and related writings.[2]

A Mysterious Oracle

The hint of a coming Messiah is found elsewhere in the five books of Moses. (Genesis, Exodus, Leviticus, Numbers, and Deuteronomy). In a strange oracle that was intended to be a curse against the people of Israel, we hear again of a coming Deliverer. King Balak feared the approaching people of Israel and hired the prophet Balaam to utter a prophecy to thwart them. But Balaam's intended curse turned into a prophetic blessing. At one point the prophet said:

> "I see him, but not now;
>> I behold him, but not near.
> A star shall come forth out of Jacob;
>> a scepter shall rise out of Israel.
> He will crush the foreheads of Moab,
>> the skulls of all the people of Sheth.
> Edom will be conquered;
>> Seir, his enemy will be conquered,
>> but Israel will grow strong.
> A ruler will come out of Jacob
>> and destroy the survivors of the city." (Numbers 24:17–19 NIV)

Balak was furious. Balaam had not cursed Israel, as he was hired to do; he had blessed Israel! But even more worrisome were the words that spoke of a coming star and scepter. Once again, these words came to be understood in reference to the awaited Messiah. The Aramaic version of the Bible translates verse 17 ("a star shall come forth out of Jacob, and a scepter shall rise out of Israel") as "a king shall come forth out of Jacob, and the Messiah will be consecrated out of Israel."[3] The oracle of Numbers 24 was widely understood to refer to the coming Messiah. It is understood this way in the Dead Sea Scrolls[4] and in early Christian writings. It is to this star that the story of the Magi ("wise men") in Matthew 2 refers. Any Jew living at the time of Jesus' birth, including the paranoid Herod the Great, would understand the significance of a reference to a strange star and a quest for the one "born king of the Jews" (Matthew 2:2).

Moses and the Law

In the book of Exodus the most famous person is Moses, the man who led the Israelites out of Egypt and gave them God's Law. Exodus narrates two great encounters with God, both involving Moses. In the first encounter God speaks to Moses from a burning bush (Exodus 3). God identifies himself as the "God of Abraham, the God of Isaac, and the God of Jacob" (3:6), whose name is Yahweh, or "He Who Is," or in the first person, "I Am Who I Am" (3:14). (In the Bible the Hebrew name *Yahweh* is usually translated "LORD.")

God then commissions Moses to go to Pharaoh, the king of Egypt, and demand that he allow the Israelites to depart. In the second encounter Moses and the people of Israel meet God at the mountain in the Sinai desert (Exodus 19–20). It is here that God gave the famous Ten Commandments (20:3–17). In short form they read as follows:

1. You shall have no other gods before me.
2. You shall not make for yourself a graven image.
3. You shall not take the name of the Lord your God in vain.
4. Remember the Sabbath day, to keep it holy.

5. Honor your father and your mother.
6. You shall not kill.
7. You shall not commit adultery.
8. You shall not steal.
9. You shall not bear false witness against your neighbor.
10. You shall not covet.

These commandments have served well the Middle East and the West for more than three thousand years.[5] Even in the East and in much of the southern hemisphere these commandments have been deeply influential and are usually regarded as authoritative. In short, the Ten Commandments provide the foundation on which human morality rests.

But this is changing rapidly in today's world. Idolatry has replaced God in many hearts and lives. People of all ages disrespectfully invoke the names of God and Jesus Christ time and again in almost every setting. We have little sense of the sacred anymore. In our culture at large there is no holy day (whether Saturday, the original Sabbath day, or Sunday, or any other day for that matter).

> The Ten Commandments provide the foundation on which human morality rests.

Parents and elders, once held in respect by society, are now looked upon as irrelevant and having nothing of value to contribute.

Even the commandments that relate to how people treat each other have lost their authoritative status. The sixth commandment forbids killing (murder), but tens of thousands of infants are aborted every year.[6] Dictators and rogue regimes murder their own citizens by the hundreds of thousands.

The seventh commandment forbids adultery, but today people jump in and out of sexual relationships with little thought of the consequences. Violence, too, is on a level that hasn't been seen for generations. Theft, lying, and coveting (prohibited by the eighth, ninth, and tenth commandments) are epidemic. Academic cheating is widespread. The financial meltdown of a few years ago brought to light a shocking level of greed and dishonesty in banks and investment firms. The public abandonment of God and of the basic ethical teachings of the Bible has created a moral sinkhole in today's society.

Second Chance at Sinai

Even the ancient Israelites, though awestruck by their experience at Sinai, found it difficult to abandon the polytheism and idolatry that their forefather Abraham had long ago rejected. While Moses was on Mount Sinai his brother, Aaron, bowed to the pressure of a fearful and superstitious people and fashioned an idol made of gold (Exodus 32). The tablets of the covenant (the stone tablets on which the Ten Commandments had been engraved) had hardly been engraved when the people broke their covenant with God. This may strike us today as incomprehensible, but Israel had grown accustomed to the gods of the Egyptians and found it difficult to give them up. Even after seeing God's power in the ten plagues he brought against Egypt—plagues that demonstrated the impotence of Pharaoh and his magicians and the nonexistence of Egypt's gods—the people of Israel still wavered in their respect for and faith in Yahweh, the God of Abraham. Idolatry is not an easy thing to give up.

Despite this grievous breach of faith, God was willing to give

Israel another chance. A new set of tablets was engraved, and Moses was permitted the opportunity to glimpse God and to hear God speak of his forgiving grace. Peering through the crack in the rock as God passed by (Exodus 33:21–23), Moses heard God say, "The LORD, the LORD, a God merciful and gracious, slow to anger, and abounding in steadfast love and faithfulness, keeping steadfast love for thousands, forgiving iniquity and transgression and sin" (34:6–7).

In this remarkable scene we learn of God's great love for humanity, even when we are fickle and faithless. I suspect many of us can identify with this remarkable experience. Despite our own failings, even betrayals, God enters our lives with grace and another chance.

Israel's idolatry was inexcusable. God had powerfully delivered them out of servitude in Egypt. In doing this God humbled the mightiest empire on earth at that time. God had shown mercy and compassion on a people of slaves (Israel), not favor for a conquering people who dominated the Middle East (Egypt). In doing this, God acted very unlike the way humans typically act.

Contrary to conventional wisdom, God had entered into a covenant with this people made up of former slaves. In this covenant God promised to give the Israelites the land he had promised Abraham long ago and to protect and care for them. Yet in a matter of days Israel violated the new covenant by making an idol and worshipping it. In doing this Israel showed herself to be no better than her pagan former masters. Nevertheless, God kept the promises he had made to Abraham, Isaac, and Jacob. He gave faithless Israel another chance. In this second chance we catch a glimpse of just how loving and forgiving God really is.

The Continuing Relevance of the Ten Commandments

How have the Ten Commandments and Israel's other laws affected Western life and society? The laws of this "old book," the Bible, have benefitted humanity in very tangible ways, ways that all of us today still experience and can appreciate.

The laws of Moses, whose principal points are summed up by the Ten Commandments, provided the rationale for a number of important advances in Western society. The moral teachings of the Bible provided the foundation on which William Wilberforce built his movement calling for an end of slavery. Shortly before he died, the British Parliament passed legislation that brought slavery to an end. In 1839 Joseph Sturge, a devout Christian and Quaker, founded the British and Foreign Anti-Slavery Society, whose mandate was to outlaw slavery throughout the world. A few decades later slavery was abolished in the United States as well. Sturge worked with the Baptists to provide homes and jobs for freed slaves.

George Williams founded the YMCA (Young Men's Christian Association) in 1844. Its sister organization, the YWCA (Young Women's Christian Association), was founded in 1855 thanks in great part to the efforts of philanthropist Lady Jane Kinnaird and Emma Robarts, a committed Christian. In their 170 years of existence the YMCA and YWCA have provided religious, educational, and physical training to countless young men and women. In the United States alone the YMCA engages some twenty-one million men, women, and children. The organization's activities led to the creation of a number of colleges and universities, including law schools, which exist and thrive to this day. The YWCA has been especially successful in advancing women's rights and creating opportunities in education and employment for women.

Raised in a Calvinist home, Henri Dunant founded the Red Cross in 1863. In 1901 he received the first Nobel Peace Prize. The International Red Cross, as its name later came to be, has provided care for millions around the world. In more recent years we think of Samaritan's Purse, a charitable organization founded in 1970 by Bob Pierce, and led today by Franklin Graham. This organization provides disaster relief, medical assistance, and clean drinking water in many of the poorest countries. Samaritan's Purse is at work in more than one hundred countries throughout the world. A great many other charities, founded on the teachings of the Bible and Christianity, work around the world to provide food, clothing, shelter, schools, and medical assistance and facilities.[7]

> These teachings may be old, but they remain very relevant, for they express great truths.

Individuals and organizations such as the ones I have briefly described were inspired by the principles enunciated by the Ten Commandments and other teachings in the Bible. These teachings may be old, but they remain very relevant, for they express great truths. When humans live by these truths, they are blessed and benefitted in tangible ways.

Prophecies

God's promise to Abraham and the great Sinai covenant between God and Israel lie behind all of the promises and many of the prophecies we read in the Old Testament. I want to focus on the prophecies centered on David, who became Israel's greatest king. I begin with a beautiful story about David's ancestors, the story of Ruth.

The Story of Ruth

In most Bibles the book of Ruth follows the book of Judges and is in turn followed by the books of Samuel. That is a good place for this story, for it fits into the final generations of the period of the judges and anticipates the beginning of Israel's rule by kings.

The book of Ruth begins with a reference to drought and famine, all-too-common occurrences in antiquity. Unlike today, in antiquity food was rarely shipped from regions of plenty to regions plagued with famine. More typically, as we have seen in the book of Genesis, people migrated from places of drought and famine in search of places where food was available. The book of Ruth tells such a story, a story about a family that left Israel—in this case the village of Bethlehem, whose name ironically means "house of bread"—to find bread in a foreign land. This family migrated to Moab, a country just southeast of Bethlehem.

The names of the family members are quite interesting and probably are meant to provide readers and hearers of this story with clues. The husband and father was Elimelech (Ruth 1:2), which means, "My God is king." His wife and mother of his sons is Naomi, which means, "pleasant." These names are quite interesting in view of what takes place in the book of Ruth. The name Elimelech may suggest that God is his king, but Elimelech left the land God had promised Abraham, a land where God was respected as Israel's true King. The name Naomi, "pleasant," recalls the Promised Land, which is mentioned in Jacob's blessing on his son Issachar: "He saw that . . . the land was *pleasant*" (Genesis 49:15; emphasis added). Having lost their confidence in God their King, Elimelech and Naomi left the Promised Land and went to Moab.

The names of Elimelech's sons foreshadowed the sorrows that

awaited the family. The name of one son was Mahlon and the other was Chilion. Although probably not their original pronunciation and meaning in the time they lived, these names in the book of Ruth mean, respectively, "sickly" and "ceasing" (as in coming to the end of life). The ancient Israelites were fond of wordplay. This is likely the case here. Israelites believed that a person's name said something about that person's character or fate.[8]

> Israelites believed that a person's name said something about that person's character or fate.

Soon things begin to go wrong. Elimelech dies (Ruth 1:3), and after taking Moabite wives the two sons of Elimelech and Naomi also die (1:4–5). Having lost her husband and two sons, the widowed, childless Naomi decides to return to Bethlehem, the "house of bread," "for she heard . . . that the LORD had visited his people in giving them bread" (1:6 ERV).

In returning to the Promised Land, Naomi is acting out repentance. In Hebrew the word used to refer to *repentance* is "return" (Hebrew: *teshuva*). We see this in the well-known parable of the prodigal son (Luke 15). When the foolish younger son comes to his senses he returns home. Naomi has heard that bread is now available in Bethlehem, so she decides to return home. But she does not yet see God's blessing. All hope seems lost.

Naomi tells her daughters-in-law, Orpah and Ruth, that she cannot give birth to more sons to be their husbands and says they will be better off as childless widows in their home country rather than as childless, widowed foreigners in the land of Israel. Naomi truly believes these women, who are still of marriageable age, will fare better in Moab. But Ruth will not separate herself from her mother-in-law. Her words of loyalty and faith are classic. She says to Naomi, "Do not urge me to leave you or to turn back from following you; for where you go, I will go, and where you lodge, I will lodge. Your people shall be my people, and your God, my God. Where you die, I will die, and there will I be buried. Thus may the LORD do to me, and worse, if anything but death parts you and me" (Ruth 1:16–17 NASB). Impressed with these words, Jewish teachers came to regard Ruth as the model convert to Israel's historic faith.

When Naomi and Ruth finally arrive at Bethlehem, the people of the village wonder, "Is this Naomi?" Perhaps they did not think the family of Elimelech would ever return. In any case, Naomi answers, "Do not call me Naomi, call me Mara, for the Almighty has dealt very bitterly with me. I went out full, but the LORD has brought me back empty" (Ruth 1:20–21 NASB). Naomi has mocked the meaning of her own name, for Mara means "bitter." Translated, she has said, "Do not call me 'Pleasant.' Instead, call me 'Bitter,' for the Almighty has dealt very bitterly with me." Naomi is bitter indeed; and she is ashamed too. She and her husband had left Bethlehem because the House of Bread lacked bread, and now she returns home empty, bereft of husband and sons. No doubt some of her former neighbors were thinking, *Serves you right!*

As it turned out, not all was lost; God had plans for Naomi and Ruth. Now landless and poor, Naomi sent Ruth out to glean among the fields (Ruth 2).[9] She sent her to fields owned by a man named Boaz, who was related to Elimelech. Boaz saw Ruth in his fields and ordered his servants to treat her well and to leave barley in the field for her to glean. He even tells her to glean nowhere else and to help herself to the food and drink provided for his servants. Ruth wonders why he shows her, a Moabite widow, such consideration. Boaz explains:

> All that you have done for your mother-in-law since the death of your husband has been fully told me, and how you left your father and mother and your native land and came to a people that you did not know before. The LORD repay you for what you have done, and a full reward be given you by the LORD, the God of Israel, under whose wings you have come to take refuge! (Ruth 2:11–12)

Boaz has heard of Ruth's kindness and devotion. His prayer is for God to reward Ruth for all she has done, for she has taken refuge under his wings. The reference to taking refuge under God's wings is ancient and expressed elsewhere in the Bible, especially in the book of Psalms. In fact, most of the psalms that speak of seeking refuge under God's wings are composed by David. Here are a few examples:

> Keep me as the apple of your eye;
> > hide me in the shadow of your wings. (Psalm 17:8)

> How precious is your steadfast love, O God!
> > The children of mankind take refuge in the shadow of your wings. (Psalm 36:7)

> Be merciful to me, O God, be merciful to me,
> > for in you my soul takes refuge;
> in the shadow of your wings I will take refuge. (Psalm 57:1)

It is intriguing that Boaz, an ancestor of David, used the same language David would use many years later.[10]

When the nearest relative of her late father-in-law refused to redeem Ruth (in keeping with the ancient law of levirate marriage), Boaz redeemed her and they were married (Ruth 4:1–13). Ruth gave birth to a son, whom Naomi nursed. Then the women of Bethlehem said to Naomi:

> Blessed be the LORD, who has not left you this day without a redeemer; and may his name be renowned in Israel! He shall be to you a restorer of life and a nourisher of your old age; for your daughter-in-law who loves you, who is more to you than seven sons, has given birth to him. (Ruth 4:14–15)

To say that Ruth, daughter-in-law of Naomi, is more to Naomi than seven sons is high praise indeed. Against all odds, Naomi, widowed and childless, has been blessed. God has rewarded her and has proven faithful. But the blessings of this happy story go way beyond the lives of Ruth and Naomi; they benefit the nation of Israel and, in the fullness of time, the entire world. Obed, the son born to Ruth, is identified as the father of Jesse, who in turn is the father of King David (Ruth 4:17, 22). Centuries later Jesus, the son of David, will be born in Bethlehem (Matthew 1:1; 2:1).

The Story of David

The beautiful story of Ruth, described by some literary critics as the world's oldest romance, illustrates God's providential care and fulfillment of his promises. In a sense the story of Ruth reaches its climax in God's covenant with King David. The youthful David had defeated the giant Goliath, had served King Saul (Israel's first king), had been anointed king by Samuel the priest and prophet, had captured Jerusalem and made it his capital, and had expanded and secured Israel's borders. Having accomplished all these things David told Nathan the prophet that he desired to build a house for God, a temple, in the city of Jerusalem (2 Samuel 7:1–3).

Although initially approving David's plans, Nathan received from God different instructions: rather than David building a house for God, God would build a house (or dynasty) for David (2 Samuel 7:4–16). God promised David that his son would be raised up as king and that God would establish this son's kingdom, as he had established David's kingdom. This son will build God's house and God will discipline him as needed (2 Samuel 7:12–15). Thus far it seems as though the prophet Nathan is only speaking of Solomon, who will in fact succeed his father David. But we begin to wonder, for in verse 16 God through his prophet goes on to say, "And your house and your kingdom shall be made sure forever before me. Your throne shall be established forever" (2 Samuel 7:16). David's kingdom ended in the Babylonian capture and destruction of Jerusalem in 586 BC. No descendant has sat on the throne of David since that time. Was God still speaking of Solomon in verse 16? Was God's covenant with David more than just a guarantee that his son Solomon would succeed him and in turn be followed by several more royal descendants from the line of David?

As early as the first century BC some Jewish interpreters believed that Nathan's prophecy had shifted from speaking about David's son Solomon to David's later descendant the Messiah.[11] The author of the New Testament book of Hebrews quotes 2 Samuel

7:14 ("I will be to him a father, and he shall be to me a son"), along with Psalm 2:7 ("You are my Son; today I have begotten you"), and applies it to Jesus, who is greater than the angels themselves (Hebrews 1:5).

The story of Ruth reaches a remarkable climax in David's enthronement as Israel's king and in God's promise that his descendant would someday rule over Israel forever. This promise was partially fulfilled in the past in the reign of Solomon and in a dynasty that endured almost four hundred years. But its ultimate fulfillment was in the coming of David's descendant Jesus, of whom the angel foretold, "The Lord God will give to him the throne of his father David, and he will reign over the house of Jacob forever, and of his kingdom there will be no end" (Luke 1:32–33).

Summing Up and Looking Ahead

Is the Bible just a bunch of dos and don'ts and negative talk? The Bible does indeed include commandments and laws—"rules," if you will—and some of them are negative. But the Bible includes a lot of the same rules and regulations we moderns have—laws against murder, theft, assault, rape, and oppression of the weak and the poor. There are also positive laws that require mercy, even generosity, toward the poor and the disadvantaged. Again, we have many of the same laws today. Indeed, much of our modern law is rooted in the Old Testament.

The Bible also contains many promises. These promises relate to humanity as a whole, but most of them center on the ancient Hebrew people, beginning with the patriarchs and matriarchs. The Bible focuses on these people, not simply because Israel is a special, chosen people, but because God has blessed and will continue to bless all of humankind through this people. The story of ancient Israel is, therefore, very important for all of us, whether Jewish or non-Jewish. Moreover, many of the promises in the Bible reveal God's character and are not necessarily tied to Israel as such. These promises make it clear that God values us and that we have a future.

God's greatest promise, which lies behind several prophecies, concerns the coming Redeemer, his Son, in fulfillment of the covenant made with David long ago. We will explore this more fully in the chapters that follow. But in the next chapter I want to mention several other promises that reveal to us God's love for us. We might call this the "bright side" of the Bible.

Why Does This Matter to Me?

- The Bible has laws, to be sure. But the purpose of these laws is to promote justice and to protect the weak and powerless. This is good for us and for our families today. If there is a downside, it is only for the selfish and the indifferent.

- The Bible also contains many promises. Some of them relate to the Jewish people. Some of them relate to humanity as a whole. But some of them relate to you and me as individuals. Knowing these promises gives us hope as we realize that our lives are in the hands of a good and loving God.

- God's promises, revealed in the Bible, show us that each one of us is important. Each one of us matters in the sight of God.

5

What's the Bright Side
of the Bible?

WHAT IS GOD LIKE? Is he a mean, angry God who insists that you follow outdated laws that are no longer relevant in today's world? Or is he a loving God who allows you to make mistakes? Or is he a distant and detached God who doesn't care about us at all? How can we know what the character of God is really like? These are good questions, and we shouldn't be afraid to ask them.

God's loving character is revealed in the promises and prophecies found in the Bible. Some of these promises relate to specific persons and specific times and places. Others relate to the nation of Israel as a whole. Some relate to all of humanity. But even when a promise or prophecy relates to a specific person, it reveals something about the character of God and so has something to teach all of us, even in our modern era. The promises in the Bible are too numerous to recount completely, so in this chapter I will review a number of important ones, grouped by general themes.

Loving Care

Through the first group of promises we learn that God has eternal concern for us. Several passages from the Psalms affirm God's loving care:

Surely goodness and mercy shall follow me all the days of
my life;
and I shall dwell in the house of the Lord forever.
(Psalm 23:6)

The Lord knows the days of the blameless,
and their heritage will abide forever. (Psalm 37:18)

But God will ransom my soul from the power of Sheol,
for he will receive me. (Psalm 49:15)

These statements affirm God's everlasting care for his people. In ourselves we are not eternal. We are born and we die. But in God we live forever. We will "dwell in the house of Lord forever." The righteous, or "blameless," will "abide forever." Our souls (or lives) will be ransomed "from the power of Sheol" (or death). God gives us strength and endurance, even as he promised a weary and discouraged Israel long ago. The prophet Isaiah tells us that God

gives power to the faint,
and to him who has no might he increases strength.
Even youths shall faint and be weary,
and young men shall fall exhausted;
but they who wait for the Lord shall renew their strength;
they shall mount up with wings like eagles;
they shall run and not be weary;
they shall walk and not faint. (Isaiah 40:29–31)

These promises are as true today as when they were spoken many centuries ago.

Jesus and his disciples confirm these promises. Jesus invited his hearers to come to him: "Come to me, all who labor and are heavy laden, and I will give you rest. Take my yoke upon you, and learn from me; for I am gentle and lowly in heart, and you will find rest for your souls" (Matthew 11:28–29). Jesus offers us the rest that we all seek, a lasting and satisfying rest that can only be found in God. Closely related to the biblical idea of rest is peace, which in Hebrew refers to being in a state of completion or wholeness. This too, Jesus offers those who follow him. Only one day before his arrest and crucifixion Jesus assured his disciples, "Peace I leave with you; my peace I give to you. Not as the world gives do I give to you. Let not your hearts be troubled, neither let them be afraid" (John 14:27). I will say more about peace shortly.

> Jesus offers us the rest that we all seek, a lasting and satisfying rest that can only be found in God.

The disciples of Jesus preached the good news of all that God had accomplished in his Son, Jesus the Messiah. Their preaching regularly referred to God's promises. Not long before his martyrdom in Rome, Peter wrote to Christians scattered about the empire, "He has granted to us his precious and very great promises, so that through them you may become partakers of the divine nature, having escaped from the corruption that is in the world because of sinful desire" (2 Peter 1:4). The apostle Paul wrote to the Christians in the city of Philippi: "And my God will supply every need of yours according to his riches in glory in Christ Jesus" (Philippians 4:19). Paul wrote these words while in prison!

Paul could write this way because of his profound conversion, in which he encountered the risen Jesus during his journey to Damascus. This was no conventional conversion by any means. Paul (or Saul, his Hebrew name) was an enemy of the early Jesus movement. His goal was to stamp it out. He was convinced that Jesus was not Israel's Messiah and certainly was not the Son of God raised from the dead, so he purposed to end the dangerous heresy before it spread further. Fortunately for all of us God had other plans for this energetic persecutor of the Church.

The book of Acts tells the story of Paul's conversion no fewer than three times (Acts 9:1–9; 22:3–21; 26:9–18), and Paul alludes to it in his letters (1 Corinthians 15:9; Galatians 1:15–17; Ephesians 3:8; Philippians 3:6; 1 Timothy 1:13). Paul's conversion transformed his understanding of himself and the world. He recognized that he could not establish his own righteousness in the sight of God. Paul's encounter with Jesus set him free, assured him that in the Messiah he was a new creation (2 Corinthians 5:17; Galatians 6:15), and gave him the peace he had been seeking his whole life (Romans 5:1; 14:17).

Paul founded several churches and wrote many letters, several of which are contained in the New Testament. These letters were addressed to specific questions and problems in first-century churches, but the issues they address remain every bit as relevant for us moderns. Today we have the same questions, face the same dilemmas, and fear many of the same things. As surely as people who lived two thousand years ago, we moderns seek assurance, respond to grace, long for forgiveness, and so forth. Let's consider several of these important things.

Assurance

After explaining the good news of what God has accomplished in his Son, Jesus—how in the Messiah all may be at peace with God and with one another—Paul bursts forth in praise:

Who shall separate us from the love of Christ? Shall trib-ulation, or distress, or persecution, or famine, or naked-ness, or peril, or sword? . . . No, in all these things we are more than conquerors through him who loved us. For I am sure that neither death nor life, nor angels nor rulers, nor things present nor things to come, nor powers, nor height nor depth, nor anything else in all creation, will be able to separate us from the love of God in Christ Jesus our Lord. (Romans 8:35, 37–39)

Paul assures the Christians in Rome and all who read his letter that nothing can separate us "from the love of Christ," and nothing can separate us "from the love of God" made available "in Christ Jesus our Lord." In this brief passage the essence of the Bible's mes-sage is summed up: God loves us, and in Christ we cannot be sepa-rated from him. This is good news indeed.

In his missionary travels Paul spoke of assurance that anyone can have in God's Son, Messiah Jesus. The apostle told an audience in Athens, God "has fixed a day on which he will judge the world in righteousness by a man whom he has appointed; and of this he has given assurance to all by raising him from the dead" (Acts 17:31). Part of this assurance is God's promise of forgiveness for anyone who asks for it.

Grace

In the Bible we frequently encounter the words *grace* and *gracious*. In the Greek New Testament the word translated "grace" is usually *charis* or a related form. This word means "unmerited favor"—to be treated much better than we deserve.

The Bible refers to grace almost two hundred times, attesting to God's grace toward humanity. Even when Israel had sinned repeatedly, "the LORD was gracious to them and had compassion on them, and he turned toward them, because of his covenant with Abraham, Isaac, and Jacob, and would not destroy them, nor has he cast them from his presence until now" (2 Kings 13:23). It is to this divine grace the psalmist refers many times, in words such as these that the Lord "is gracious, merciful, and righteous" (Psalm 112:4; see also Psalms 111:4; 116:5; 135:3). Jesus thanks God for revealing his truth to the disciples, for such was God's "gracious will" (Matthew 11:26 and Luke 10:21). James assures his readers that God "gives grace to the humble" (James 4:6), while Paul finds God's grace in the "free gift" he offers all humanity in his Son, Jesus (Romans 5:15). This is why Paul can speak of the "immeasurable riches of [God's] grace in kindness toward us in Christ Jesus" and then declare, "By grace you have been saved through faith. And this is not your own doing; it is the gift of God" (Ephesians 2:7–8).

Perhaps the most moving example of divine grace is found in a passage in Exodus. After Israel's dreadful violation of the covenant that had just been ratified at Sinai, God shows grace and gives his people a second chance. He shows himself to Moses, saying, "The LORD, the LORD, a God merciful and gracious, slow to anger, and abounding in steadfast love and faithfulness" (Exodus 34:6). These words left a deep impression on Israel. We hear them echoed in the Psalms and in the prophets:

> But you, O Lord, are a God merciful and gracious,
>   slow to anger and abounding in steadfast love and faith-
> fulness. (Psalm 86:15)

The LORD is merciful and gracious,
   slow to anger and abounding in steadfast love. (Psalm 103:8)

The LORD is gracious and merciful,
   slow to anger and abounding in steadfast love. (Psalm 145:8)

Return to the LORD your God,
   for he is gracious and merciful,
slow to anger, and abounding in steadfast love,
   and relents over disaster. (Joel 2:13)

The apostle John alludes to Exodus 34:6 in his famous prologue: "And the Word became flesh, and dwelt among us, . . . full of grace and truth" (John 1:14 NASB). John's "full of grace and truth" is the Greek equivalent of the Hebrew phrase "abounding in steadfast love and faithfulness." John is implying that the supreme grace of God witnessed on Mount Sinai long ago foreshadowed the grace of God in the coming of his Son, Jesus. In Jesus this divine grace has become flesh.

The grace of God is what makes forgiveness possible. For faithless and feckless humanity, God's promise of forgiveness may well be his most important promise of all.

Forgiveness

Because God is loving and gracious, he forgives, removes guilt, and cleanses the human heart. The prophet Isaiah urges the wicked to repent:

Let the wicked forsake their ways,
  and the unrighteous their thoughts.
Let them turn to the Lord, and he will have mercy on
them,
  and to our God, for he will freely pardon. (Isaiah 55:7 NIV)

No matter how estranged from God, no matter how wicked, everyone who turns to God will receive mercy and be pardoned. Indeed, our record will be expunged, as both Isaiah and Jeremiah declare:

I, I am he
  who blots out your transgressions for my own sake,
and I will not remember your sins. (Isaiah 43:25)

I will forgive their iniquity, and I will remember their sin
no more. (Jeremiah 31:34)

It may seem strange to think that God, who knows all that can be known, can somehow no longer remember our sin. Of course, the point is not simply divine amnesia. In the Bible to speak of "remembering" something usually implies taking action—that is, recalling what someone has done and then acting accordingly. When God says he will not remember our sin, he means that he will not hold us to account. When we repent, we are forgiven and our sin is no longer charged against us. Our slate is wiped clean.

Our sin, the Bible tells us, is removed "as far as the east is from the west, so far does [God] remove our transgressions from us" (Psalm 103:12). Indeed, according to the prophet Micah, God will cast all our sins "into the depths of the sea" (Micah 7:19). It is no wonder that the psalmist praises God, saying, "For You, O LORD, are good and forgiving, abounding in steadfast love to all who call upon you" (Psalm 86:5). God is not petty or mean-spirited. He holds no grudges. He desires the best for us. God desires us to know him and to live in harmony with one another and with the beautiful world he has made for us.

Jesus spoke often of forgiveness, exhorting his followers to forgive one another (Matthew 18:21–22, 35; Mark 11:25). In his well-known Lord's Prayer, Jesus asks God to forgive us just as we forgive those who have sinned against us (Matthew 6:12). Jesus taught that in his death on the cross forgiveness will be made available to anyone who appeals to God (Matthew 26:28). Jesus forgave sinners (Mark 2:5; Luke 7:47–48) and even forgave those who put him to death (Luke 23:34). His parable of the two debtors (Matthew 18:23–35) illustrates how God has forgiven us and how we in turn ought to forgive those who have wronged us. The parable of the prodigal son (Luke 15:11–32) offers yet another moving example of forgiveness.

Following their Master's teaching and example the disciples proclaimed forgiveness (Acts 2:38; 5:31; 10:43; 13:38; 26:18; Romans 4:7; Ephesians 1:7; Colossians 2:13; 3:13). Stephen, who suffered martyrdom, forgave those who desired his death (Acts 7:60).

Though these teachings about forgiveness were uttered long ago, they are very relevant today to you and me.

Fulfillment

In the Bible God also promises to fulfill our desires. God "has satisfied the thirsty soul, and the hungry soul He has filled with what is good" (Psalm 107:9 NASB). The psalmist promises, "The afflicted shall eat and be satisfied; those who seek him will praise the LORD! May your hearts live forever!" (Psalm 22:26). And, "You satisfy the desire of every living thing" (Psalm 145:15–16). Far from being an ogre and killjoy, God wishes the best for humanity. The psalmist knows this and so exhorts, "Delight yourself in the LORD, and he will give you the desires of your heart" (Psalm 37:4).

The prophets, too, know that God loves his people and provides for them. Isaiah challenges on God's behalf, "Why do you spend your money for that which is not bread, and your labor for that which does not satisfy? Listen diligently to me, and eat what is good, and delight yourselves in rich food" (Isaiah 55:2). Jeremiah agrees, adding, "'My people shall be satisfied with my goodness,' declares the LORD" (Jeremiah 31:14). So does the prophet Joel, who speaks for God, "You will have plenty to eat and be satisfied and praise the name of the LORD your God, who has dealt wondrously with you; then My people will never be put to shame" (Joel 2:26 NASB).

God's will for humanity is generous and loving, but sinful humans divert or withhold many of his gifts, even basic ones like food and water. We think of famine in Africa or violence in the Middle East, in which the innocent suffer, including children. This is not God's will. These tragedies underscore that people desperately need to hear and heed God's message of love and reconciliation. The need today is as great as it has ever been. We have made great progress in science, technology, travel, and communication—yet in ignoring God we continue to bring upon ourselves many of the problems that our ancestors faced.

Hope

When we recognize God's goodness and provision, we have a reason to have hope. But without God, do we have any grounds for hope? Atheist Richard Dawkins doesn't think so: "The universe we observe has precisely the properties we should expect if there is, at bottom, no design, no purpose, no evil and no good, nothing but blind, pitiless indifference."[1] What a dismal perspective. Alas, Dawkins is not alone in expressing such hopelessness. Another atheist, philosopher Bertrand Russell, opined that humanity's existence is mere chance, with no purpose and ultimately no future. Only on this "firm foundation of unyielding despair, can the soul's habitation henceforth be safely built."[2] Contemporary philosopher Thomas Nagel, adding to this bleak assessment of the human condition, declares that "life as a whole is meaningless."[3]

This is where atheism leads, when understood properly and consistently thought out.[4] It leads to utter hopelessness. Without God there is no hope.

In contrast, the Bible speaks of hope throughout its pages. Drawing on his deep experience of God, the psalmist speaks of hope and praises God for making hope possible.

> Why are you cast down, O my soul,
>> and why are you in turmoil within me?
> Hope in God; for I shall again praise him,
>> my salvation and my God. (Psalm 42:11)

> Be strong, and let your heart take courage,
>> all you who wait for the Lord! (Psalm 31:24)

For You, O LORD, are my hope,

my trust, O LORD, from my youth. (Psalm 71:5)

The prophet Jeremiah shared this hope, which was confirmed in his vision of God. This enabled him to offer hope to his people, who saw the kingdom of David coming to an end: "For I know the plans I have for you, declares the LORD, plans for welfare and not for evil, to give you a future and a hope" (Jeremiah 29:11).

Jesus' teaching and astounding works of supernatural power energized his disciples and renewed their hope that the God of Israel was indeed a keeper of his promises. The resurrection removed any lingering doubt: Israel's hope in God was not in vain. The promises God had made long ago to the patriarchs and the prophecies uttered by Israel's prophets were fulfilled in Jesus' resurrection. This is the substance of Peter's preaching on the Day of Pentecost, the day that gave birth to the Church.

When Peter announces the resurrection of Jesus, he appeals to Psalm 16. In this Psalm David speaks of his confidence that God will not abandon his descendant, the Messiah, in the grave, nor allow his body to decay. Because David is dead and his tomb is present in Jerusalem, Peter reasons rightly that David was not speaking of himself but was looking ahead to the resurrection of the Messiah. This prophecy was fulfilled in the resurrection of Jesus (Acts 2:24–31). Because of the promise of resurrection, says David, his "flesh"—that is, his moral self—"will dwell in hope" (Acts 2:26, quoting Psalm 16:9, according to the Greek version). Today, we have hope because our

> The resurrection removed any lingering doubt: Israel's hope in God was not in vain.

existence does not come to an end with the death of our bodies. We know this hope rests on a firm foundation because of the fulfillment of David's prophecy in the resurrection of his descendant Jesus the Messiah.

Good News

The resurrection of Jesus is why Peter boldly preaches the good news, even when persecuted (Acts 4:1–22; 5:17–42). Late in life Peter continues to proclaim the resurrection and speak of hope (1 Peter 1:3, 13, 21). Paul, too, links hope and resurrection in his speeches in Acts and in his letters. When brought before the Jewish court in Jerusalem, Paul cries out, "I am a Pharisee, a son of Pharisees. It is with respect to the hope and the resurrection of the dead I am on trial" (Acts 23:6). Paul identifies himself as a Pharisee because the Pharisees believed in resurrection.

Without the resurrection there is no hope. This is why the resurrection of Jesus, which startled his confused disciples on Easter Sunday and utterly altered the aggressive Paul on the road to Damascus, was so important for the Jesus movement. It was not the superb teaching of Jesus, or even his amazing works of power; it was his resurrection. With Jesus' resurrection it was now possible to speak of real hope—hope in the time of the early Church and hope in our own time.

This is wonderful news, wouldn't you agree? Down through the centuries humans have wondered what, if anything, lies beyond the grave. In the resurrection of Jesus, this pressing question has been answered in an affirming and assuring way. To join Jesus is to join in his resurrection. We need not fear death ever again.

Paul returns to the theme of hope and resurrection time and

again. When standing before Felix, the Roman governor of Israel (ruled AD 52–60), Paul declares that he serves God, "having a hope in God which these [Christians] themselves accept, that there will be a resurrection of both the just and the unjust" (Acts 24:15). Later still, standing before King Agrippa II (ruled AD 44–66), Paul says, "And now I stand here on trial because of my hope in the promise made by God to our fathers, to which our twelve tribes hope to attain, as they earnestly worship night and day. And for this hope I am accused by Jews, O king!" (Acts 26:6–7). Three times in this passage the word "hope" appears. According to Paul, the hope of resurrection began with the promise God gave Abraham long ago, a hope that the twelve tribes of Israel embraced, and now a hope fulfilled in the resurrection of Jesus (Acts 26:8). "Since we have such a hope," Paul says, "we are very bold" (2 Corinthians 3:12).

> The Bible promises that those who seek God will have peace.

The good news of Jesus was foretold by the prophet Isaiah, who spoke of the coming rule of God:

> Go on up to a high mountain,
>   O Zion, herald of good news;
> lift up your voice with strength,
>   O Jerusalem, herald of good news,
>   lift it up, fear not;
> say to the cities of Judah,
>   "Behold your God!" (Isaiah 40:9)

> How beautiful upon the mountains
>   are the feet of him who brings good news,

who publishes peace, who brings good news of happiness,
    who publishes salvation,
    who says to Zion, "Your God reigns." (Isaiah 52:7)

The Spirit of the Lord GOD is upon me,
    because the LORD has anointed me
to bring good news to the poor,
    he has sent me to bind up the brokenhearted,
to proclaim liberty to the captives,
    and the opening of the prison to those who are bound;
to proclaim the year of the LORD's favor. (Isaiah 61:1–2)

Bible scholars recognize that these passages and others like them lie behind Jesus' proclamation of the kingdom of God, a theme that will be explored more fully in chapter 7. For now it is important to understand that the promises of the Bible are closely tied to the promised good news, a promise that would be fulfilled in the coming of Jesus. This good news and its fulfillment provide the foundation for another important promise: peace.

Peace

The Bible promises that those who seek God will have peace, that wonderful Hebrew word (*shalom*) that means completion and wholeness. The psalmist prays, "May the LORD give strength to his people! May the LORD bless his people with peace!" (Psalm 29:11). The grammar of this verse is such that it could read this way: "The Lord will give strength to his people; the Lord will bless his people with peace."

Although troubled by his people's wickedness and impending

judgment, the prophet Isaiah was confident that God's peace was still in Israel's future: "O Lord, you will ordain peace for us, for you have indeed done for us all our works" (Isaiah 26:12).

We have already observed that Isaiah spoke of the good news of peace. He also spoke of the bringer of this peace, a Prince of Peace. He speaks of this Prince in a time of fear and doubt about the line of King David. His descendants had hardly proven to be faithful. Would this royal line come to an end? Would God's promise given through Nathan the prophet go unfulfilled? Not at all. Isaiah uttered these words, which are recalled every year in the Christmas season:

> For to us a child is born,
>   to us a son is given;
> and the government shall be upon his shoulder,
>   and his name shall be called
> Wonderful Counselor, Mighty God,
>   Everlasting Father, Prince of Peace.
> Of the increase of his government and of peace
>   there will be no end,
> on the throne of David, and over his kingdom,
>   to establish it, and to uphold it
> with justice and with righteousness
>   from this time forth and forevermore.
> The zeal of the Lord of hosts will do this. (Isaiah 9:6–7)

Through his prophet God promised humanity a son who will be called "Wonderful Counselor, Mighty God, Everlasting Father,

Prince of Peace." Christians believe that this great promise and prophecy was fulfilled in Jesus of Nazareth, who comforted his disciples with these words: "Peace I leave with you; my peace I give to you. Not as the world gives do I give to you. Let not your hearts be troubled, neither let them be afraid" (John 14:27). The Prince of Peace offers peace to all who receive him.

This great truth is reflected in the apostles' teaching. Paul encourages the faithful in Philippi:

> Do not be anxious about anything, but in everything by prayer and supplication with thanksgiving let your requests be made known to God. And the peace of God, which passes all understanding, will keep your hearts and your minds in Christ Jesus. (Philippians 4:6–7)

Paul exhorts believers, "What you have learned and received and heard and seen in me—practice these things, and the God of peace will be with you" (Philippians 4:9). The God of the Bible is a God of peace. But this peace is a personal, relational peace. This is why Paul affirms that Jesus, God's Son, becomes "our peace" (Ephesians 2:14). After clarifying the human condition of estrangement and how in God's grace and mercy we may be forgiven, Paul declares, "Therefore, since we are justified by faith, we have peace with God through our Lord Jesus Christ" (Romans 5:1). When we are reconciled to God by his grace, which we receive through faith, we have peace with God. Billy Graham well understood this great truth when he penned his classic book, *Peace with God.*[5]

Wisdom

The Bible also promises wisdom to those who ask for it. God is described as a Teacher. The psalmist thanks God for his instruction (Psalms 71:17; 119:102), which includes wisdom (Psalm 51:6). Some of the writings in the Bible are classified as books of wisdom. These include Ecclesiastes, Proverbs, Job, and the Song of Solomon. In Ecclesiastes the Preacher asserts, "God gives wisdom" to those who please him (Ecclesiastes 2:26). According to Proverbs 2:65, "the Lord gives wisdom." God teaches the faithful the "way of wisdom" (Proverbs 4:11). The prophet Isaiah foresees a time when all people will seek God, desiring to be taught his ways (Isaiah 2:3). It will be a time when all will be "taught by the Lord" (Isaiah 54:13).

Jesus invites people to come to him and to learn from him (Matthew 11:28–29). Years later James, the half brother of Jesus, writes to the believers scattered throughout the Roman Empire, "If any of you lacks wisdom, let him ask God, who gives generously to all without reproach, and it will be given him" (James 1:5). People have been requesting and receiving God's wisdom from Bible times to today.

Summing Up and Looking Ahead

Critics of the Bible often focus on the laws that prohibit certain behavior. They also point out the violence, wars, bloodshed, and the like. But these critics often overlook the many promises of the Bible—healing, restorative counsel, assurance, hope, and forgiveness. Lying behind all of these positives are the goodness and graciousness of God.

Ancient Israel enjoyed many of these positive promises. Although a small nation, Israel established a kingdom that flourished for almost half a millennium—a remarkable achievement. Unfortunately God's people do not always remember God's promises, and they do not always heed his laws and warnings. When they do not, problems inevitably result. To those problems we turn in the next chapter.

Why Does This Matter to Me?

❋ The promises of the Bible reveal the goodness and mercy of God. They show us that God really does care about us. That is wonderful news that can transform our self-image, sense of purpose, and lives today.

❋ The promises of God are not pie in the sky but relevant, needed, and very down-to-earth—where you and I live.

❋ Many people have experienced the reality of God's promises. They have experienced God's promised grace and forgiveness. Above all, they have experienced the promised peace that only God can provide. When we know the God of the Bible, who makes those promises, you and I can experience those things too.

6

What Happens If
We Ignore the Bible?

AT THE ZENITH of the kingdom of Israel, the nation had come into possession of her Promised Land, had established the city of Jerusalem as the capital, had built a beautiful temple, and had seen considerable growth in population. The land, posterity, and blessing God had promised Abraham were now a reality.

The high point of this Jewish Camelot was the rule of Solomon, David's son and Israel's wise and famous king. It was Solomon who built the temple, sparing no cost (1 Kings 5–7), and when it was completed he dedicated it with great ceremony (1 Kings 8). God repeated the covenant he had made with Solomon's father, David, that someday he would have a son who would sit on the throne. But God also warned Solomon of the dire consequences if he or his descendants should forsake God and chase after the gods and idols of the nations (1 Kings 9:4–9). Sadly, these words of warning would eventually come to pass.

The nation's moral slide affected every level of society. Israel's kings abused the power entrusted to them. They paid homage to other gods as part of their treaties with nearby nations. The wealthy oppressed the poor and powerless. The ruling priests became corrupt, accepting bribes and indulging in polytheism. Even the lower classes ignored God and held back their support for the temple and for the widows and orphans. Many prophets rose up and spoke against these abuses, but often they suffered at the hands of the rulers and the people.

How Do the Ten Commandments Apply Today?

As I said before, some people today view the Ten Commandments as legalistic and irrelevant. Maybe you have thought that too. Who needs those old rules today? This is a good time to say more about their original intention. The Ten Commandments, along with many of the other laws in the Law of Moses, were not intended to impose a bunch of legalistic rules on people, to make their lives harder and less fun. Far from it. Let's run through them again, this time applying them to the realities of life, especially life in the ancient Near East.

The first two Commandments prohibit polytheism and idolatry:

You shall have no other gods before me.
You shall not make for yourself a carved image. (Exodus 20:3–4)

God requires his people to worship him and him alone. To worship "other gods" presupposes polytheism. Polytheism, which divides God into many, enables people to do almost anything in the name of one god or another. It allows people to justify violence and oppression ("Our god is at war with your god," and so forth). God's prohibition against polytheism frees people from the bondage of superstition, of trying to appease several gods, even playing one god against another.

In polytheism, God becomes "my god," as opposed to "your god." The mind-set is, "My god only cares about me and my people; he has no regard or concern for you and your people." The prophets of Israel saw the folly in this and boldly declared that God is the God *of all*; he cares for the Gentiles as much as he does for the people of Israel. Such a vision of God was unheard of in the ancient Near East, at least outside of Israel.

Closely related to polytheism is idolatry. Making idols, housing them, praying to them, cleaning them, even "feeding" them, only added to the temptation to domesticate God. With an idol placed somewhere in your home, you are tempted to think that you can train, in a sense control, your god. Idols are an insult to God, as if an artisan could capture his image. This is why there was no image of God in Israel's temple. There was a mercy seat, on which God symbolically sat, but no image of God himself.

The first two commandments, which prohibited polytheism and the production of "graven images," (engraved images of gods, animals, and the like), were in fact a benefit, not a narrow-minded limitation preventing Israel from being "ecumenical" with respect to the gods and idols of their pagan neighbors. Polytheism not only divides God, but it also divides humanity. Israel was to be a witness to other nations, showing them a better way. This is why in his dedication of the temple Solomon asks God to hear the prayers of the non-Israelites who come to Jerusalem (1 Kings 8:48–49). This is ecumenism rightly understood: the God of Israel is One (Deuteronomy 6:4), and all who approach him with sincere hearts are welcome.

The third commandment prohibits misuse of God's name: "You shall not take the name of the LORD your God in vain" (Exodus 20:7). Many people think this commandment prohibits foul language. Actually, this commandment only indirectly relates to swearing. The prohibition to take the name of God "in vain" was intended to prevent false oaths invoking God's name. In antiquity it was common for people to appeal to this god or that god, or a whole host of gods, in swearing an oath. But often these oaths were a deceitful attempt to commit fraud or worse.

In the time of Jesus people swore oaths by appealing to God, the temple, the gold on the temple, or whatever. And just as often these oaths could be disqualified or rescinded altogether on the grounds of some technicality. This kind of talk cheapens the name of God and all that is sacred. This is why Jesus teaches his disciples to answer truthfully, to say yes or no and not swear on this or that, in order to equivocate or create a loophole (Matthew 5:33–37).

False oaths defrauded the poor and the powerless—and this was done in God's name! The third commandment prohibits this practice and in doing so protects the poor and the powerless.

The fourth commandment requires God's people to "remember the Sabbath day, to keep it holy" (Exodus 20:8). Again, the purpose of this commandment was not to place restrictions on people to make their lives more difficult. The point was to free up people, to prevent rulers and employers from forcing people to work every day of the week. The Sabbath principle was supremely compassionate. People need rest; they need to take time off. But there was a religious purpose too. Ceasing from daily work gives us time to meditate, to worship, and to think about the big questions, the kinds of questions the Bible addresses. Observing a Sabbath day gives us the opportunity to ask ourselves who we are and why we are here. The break from a hectic workweek allows us time to think about God.

The fifth commandment, "Honor your father and mother" (Exodus 20:12), was designed to protect elderly parents and to preserve and strengthen a vital part of social structure. Humans, unlike animals in the wild, care for the elderly, weak, and infirm. Sometimes the fifth commandment is understood in a limited way, as though its point was to encourage children to speak to their parents respectfully or to obey. This is part of it, but the important point was that children were to care for their aging parents. In antiquity children were their parents' retirement plan.

> The Law of Moses was a huge step forward in protecting the poor and weak.

This helps us understand why Jesus was so critical of religious teachers of his day who declared their personal property "Qorban" (meaning a gift dedicated to God) and then could no longer assist their parents. In doing this, Jesus taught, these teachers had violated the fifth commandment (Mark 7:1–23).

The sixth commandment, "You shall not kill," which primarily referred to murder (Exodus 20:13), may strike us all today as rather obvious. But the original purpose was to protect the weak from the powerful. In antiquity ideas of justice and human rights were in their infancy. The Law of Moses was a huge step forward in protecting the poor and weak. The commandment not to kill was intended primarily to hold the powerful in check.

The seventh commandment, "You shall not commit adultery" (Exodus 20:14), may strike some modern people as antiquated. What consenting adults do is their business, right? But the original purpose had as much to do with protecting the weak from the strong as it had to do with morality in our modern sense. Just because a man was wealthy and powerful, even a king, did not mean that he could take another man's wife.

The eighth commandment, "You shall not steal" (Exodus 20:15), again seems obvious to us. Who could object to it? But this commandment was necessary to protect people from those who abused their positions of power.

The ninth commandment, "You shall not bear witness against your neighbor" (Exodus 20:16), was designed to protect the innocent from slander and perjury. False testimony could be used as a weapon against a rival or as a way for someone to avoid the punishment he deserves. The ninth commandment also discouraged bribery and other attempts to subvert justice.

The tenth commandment, "You shall not covet" (Exodus 20:17), is an interesting one indeed. There is no law in the modern world, of which I am aware, that prohibits coveting. Why should there be such a law? The Law of Moses wisely prohibits coveting because many evils begin with coveting. The desire for someone's property could lead to theft and murder and perhaps also to false testimony. The desire for another person's spouse could lead to adultery. The tenth commandment, in a sense, serves as a safeguard to prevent the violation of commandments six through nine.

What Happens When People Don't Follow the Ten Commandments?

The Old Testament offers us two graphic examples of how the Ten Commandments were designed primarily to protect the weak and powerless. In both cases the problem began with coveting.

King Ahab and Queen Jezebel

The first example concerns King Ahab and his infamous wife, Queen Jezebel. Ahab was the king of the northern half of Israel, called Samaria. As an Israelite, Ahab knew the Law of Moses, and he perfectly well knew the sixth commandment, which prohibited murder. But Jezebel was a pagan, the daughter of the king of Sidon. The Law of Moses, including the Ten Commandments, meant very little to her.

Trouble began when Ahab coveted a vineyard owned by a man named Naboth. He asked Naboth if he could buy the vineyard. Naboth refused, because the vineyard had been in the family for generations (1 Kings 21). The vineyard was on Naboth's family's original estate, perhaps going all the way back to the time of Joshua and the apportioning of land to the Israelites. Selling this land to anyone, even the king, was unthinkable.

His bid rejected, Ahab was downcast. Jezebel observed this and asked, "Why is your spirit so vexed that you eat no food?" (1 Kings 21:5). How childish. Evidently Ahab was used to getting his way. And why not? He was the king, after all. So what held Ahab in check? The Law of Moses. He could not simply seize Naboth's land. If Naboth would not sell it, then that settled it. But not so in the thinking of Jezebel. "Do you now govern Israel?" she asked her husband (1 Kings 21:5). Where she comes from, the king takes whatever he wants. "I will give you the vineyard of Naboth," she promised. And she did. Jezebel arranged to have Naboth accused of having cursed God and the king, resulting in his execution. Ahab then took possession of the vineyard (1 Kings 21:8–17).

This ugly episode was scandalous. Jezebel and Ahab suborned

perjury and committed murder and theft, thus violating the sixth, eighth, and ninth commandments. And this whole sorry train of events had begun with Ahab coveting Naboth's property, a violation of the tenth commandment.

Had this occurred in the kingdom of Sidon, the king and queen would have gotten away with it—but not in Israel. It wasn't long before Ahab was confronted by Elijah the prophet, who warned the king that God would judge him for his crime. In time, that judgment came. Both Ahab and Jezebel died in dishonor.

The role Elijah played in this drama illustrates for us the role that Israel's prophets frequently played in the nation. If I may draw an analogy to Canada's parliamentary system of government, Israel's prophets functioned as the "loyal opposition" to the government. The prophet's loyalty was to God, not to the royal government. When the government stepped out of line, the prophet challenged the government. When the king sinned, the prophet confronted him about it.

David and Bathsheba

One of the most dramatic encounters between a prophet and a king in Israel is seen in the story of King David's affair with Bathsheba, the wife of Uriah the Hittite (2 Samuel 11).

The story begins with David catching a glimpse of a woman bathing. Because the king's palace was the tallest building in Jerusalem, the king could look down upon his city. This was especially so if he were up on the roof (2 Samuel 11:2). From this vantage point David saw a beautiful woman bathing and asked about her. Thus far David has done nothing wrong. In his time wealthy men had more than one wife and kings were no exception.

Where David goes wrong was when he learned that the woman was Bathsheba, wife of David's soldier Uriah, he took her anyway and had sex with her. David could not marry her, for she already was married. The Bible does not say that David raped Bathsheba, but given his royal power and the woman's powerlessness it almost amounts to the same thing. Some time later Bathsheba discovered she was pregnant and informed David. The king then tried to get Uriah to return home and spend time with his wife so Uriah would think the baby was his own, but Uriah declined to sleep with his wife. Did Uriah suspect? We will never know. In desperation David arranged Uriah's murder by placing him in an impossible position on the field of battle.

In doing this wicked deed David violated several of the Ten Commandments. He coveted and lusted after another man's wife. In effect he stole Bathsheba from Uriah. David committed adultery. He lied. He committed murder. He involved some of his servants and soldiers in this crime. David had violated commandments six through ten. After he learned of Uriah's death, he consoled the grieving widow by adding her to his harem. David thought he had gotten away with it, but he was very wrong.

Another king in another kingdom could have gotten away with it, but not in Israel. Soon Nathan the prophet appeared before David. This was the same Nathan who had uttered the oracle about David's dynasty and special descendant (2 Samuel 7). But this time Nathan had a very different message. He began with a story:

There were two men in a certain city, the one rich and the other poor. The rich man had very many flocks and herds, but the poor man had nothing but one little ewe lamb, which he had bought. And he brought it up, and it grew up with him and with his children. It used to eat of his morsel and drink from his cup and lie in his arms, and it was like a daughter to him. Now there came a traveler to the rich man, and he was unwilling to take one of his own flock or herd to prepare for the guest who had come to him, but he took the poor man's lamb and prepared it for the man who had come to him. (2 Samuel 12:1–4)

David assumes that Nathan is reporting an actual event, in which a powerful, wealthy man has taken advantage of a poor neighbor. When David hears the story, he is outraged. No one gets away with this kind of thing on his watch! David assures Nathan, "As the LORD lives, the man who has done this deserves to die, and he shall restore the lamb fourfold, because he did this thing, and because he had no pity" (2 Samuel 12:5–6).

David's assertion that the rich man should compensate the poor man fourfold reflects the Law of Moses, where thieves are required to make fourfold restitution (Exodus 22:1). And although the rich man has only stolen a lamb, David nevertheless thinks the man deserves death, so callous is his deed!

We hear in David's righteous anger the judgment of a king who knows the Law of Moses and normally respects and obeys it. David often referred to the Law of Moses or "the law of the Lord" in the psalms he wrote:

The law of the LORD is perfect,
    reviving the soul;

the testimony of the LORD is sure,
  making wise the simple. (Psalm 19:7)

Blessed are those whose way is blameless,
  who walk in the law of the LORD! (Psalm 119:1)

In Psalm 5 David gives forceful expression to his commitment to justice and the divine law on which it is based:

For You are not a God who delights in wickedness;
  evil may not dwell with you.
The boastful shall not stand before your eyes;
  you hate all evildoers.
You destroy those who speak lies;
  the LORD abhors the bloodthirsty and deceitful man.
But I, through the abundance of your steadfast love,
  will enter your house.
I will bow down toward your holy temple
  in the fear of you. (Psalm 5:4–7)

Nathan the prophet likely knew David was a good king who ruled his people fairly and under the guidance of the Law of Moses. But David was a man nonetheless and as such was capable of sin. David had done a wicked thing and had tried to cover it up. But all was known to Nathan, God's prophet.

To David's great surprise he learns that the story Nathan has told him was a juridical parable, in which the unsuspecting hearer passes judgment on himself. Had Nathan approached David and told him he knew what the king had done, David likely would have made excuses or lied or blamed Bathsheba or someone else. But because Nathan told the king a story—which the king didn't think concerned him directly—David pronounced a righteous judgment. "The man who has done this deserves to die," David said. Readers and hearers of this story wonder: If a man who stole a neighbor's animal deserves to die, then what about a man who stole a neighbor's wife and then murdered the neighbor?

Before David's righteous anger can cool, Nathan reveals the mind of God in this matter:

> "You are the man! Thus says the LORD, the God of Israel, 'I anointed you king over Israel, and I delivered you out of the hand of Saul. And I gave you your master's house, and your master's wives into your arms, and gave you the house of Israel and of Judah. And if this were too little, I would add to you as much more. Why have you despised the word of the LORD, to do what is evil in his sight? You have struck down Uriah the Hittite with the sword, and have taken his wife to be your wife, and have killed him with the sword of the Ammonites. Now therefore the sword shall never depart from your house, because you have despised me, and have taken the wife of Uriah the Hittite to be your wife.' Thus says the LORD, 'Behold, I will raise up evil against you out of your own house. And I will take your wives before your eyes, and give them to your neighbor, and he shall lie with your wives in the sight of this sun. For you did it secretly; but I will do this thing before all Israel, and before the sun.'" (2 Samuel 12:7–12)

Nathan's words bring home the gravity of David's sin. After all that God had done for him, what does David do? He murders Uriah and takes his wife as one of his own. In doing these things David has "despised the word of the Lord," the Law of Moses. As king of Israel, David is to model the righteousness of God and to set an example for the nation. In one sinful episode David has violated half of the Ten Commandments.

To David's credit he does not offer any excuses. He blames no one but himself. He confesses, "I have sinned against the LORD." Because of this confession, Nathan was able to assure David, "The LORD also has put away your sin; you shall not die" (2 Samuel 12:13). David was forgiven, but his sinful deeds had terrible and lasting consequences for his family and for the nation.

> David was forgiven, but his sinful deeds had terrible and lasting consequences for his family and for the nation.

The abuses of power we see in Ahab and David are not too different from what we see in the rich, famous, and powerful of our time. From pop stars to politicians we have seen many fall, having broken one or more of the Ten Commandments. Celebrity athletes have cheated with performance-enhancing drugs, have committed acts of violence against women, and even in one case a star football player has been charged with murder. We were stunned by the massive fraud perpetrated by Bernie Madoff, who stole billions of dollars from people and institutions that had placed their trust in him.

In our world the Ten Commandments and the ethical principles taught in the Bible are far from obsolete. They remain as relevant as ever. Had they been heeded, the crimes and tragedies that have overtaken many successful men and women would not have happened. What will it take for people today to wake up?

The Role of Prophets in Israel

In the four-hundred-year history of the kingdom of Israel, while some of Israel's kings were good, most followed the examples of the pagan rulers in the Middle East. Typically Israel's kings would form alliances or sign treaties with their pagan neighbors, which required showing respect to the gods and idols of the pagans. Sometimes foreign influence led to immoral practices, such as temple prostitution, or to abominable practices, such as child sacrifice and various forms of witchcraft.

It is against this checkered history of Israel that the activities of the prophets should be understood. The prophets applied the Law of Moses to society, often harshly criticizing the wealthy and ruling elite. This almost always was presented as a warning: If you don't change your ways, if you don't stop cheating the poor, the orphan, the widow, etc., then the Lord will bring judgment. You will lose your wealth, you will be taken captive, etc. Sometimes the prophets speak words of comfort, promising a beleaguered nation that God will redeem them and restore them. It is in this context that prophecies concerning the coming Messiah usually appear. Most people focus on these prophecies, but in reality they represent only a small percentage of the message of the prophets.

One of my favorite passages in the Prophets is found in Micah, who was active in the eighth century BC. He warns the wealthy who think that they can persuade God to overlook their crimes by bringing expensive gifts to the temple in Jerusalem. Here is what the prophet says:

"With what shall I come before the LORD,
  and bow myself before God on high?
Shall I come before him with burnt offerings,
  with calves a year old?
Will the LORD be pleased with thousands of rams,
  with ten thousands of rivers of oil?
Shall I give my firstborn for my transgression,
  the fruit of my body for the sin of my soul?"
He has told you, O man, what is good;
  and what does the LORD require of you
but to do justice, and to love kindness,
  and to walk humbly with your God? (Micah 6:6–8)

The double-commandment to love God and love our neighbors is echoed in these words, especially in the last verse (v. 8). "What does the LORD require?" "To do justice, and to love kindness." That is, to do justice toward our neighbors (especially the poor) and to extend kindness to those who are in need. The last phrase, "to walk humbly with God," echoes the command to love God. We see that God does not want expensive gifts or bribes; he wants us to show mercy and walk humbly. Can you imagine how transformed the world would be if everyone followed these words? Can you imagine how your own life would be transformed if you embraced the word of God as spoken through the prophet Micah? If you followed this word, what would it do for you as a friend, spouse, parent, or employer?

The most respected prophet in the Old Testament was Isaiah. His book was cited more than any other book of prophecy by Jesus, by the writers of the New Testament, by the ancient rabbis, and by the men of Qumran who collected and wrote many of the Dead Sea Scrolls. Though Isaiah was by far the most popular of the prophets in later generations, he was not popular with the ruling elite during his own time.

Isaiah was hard-hitting. He fearlessly confronted kings and no-bility. He advocated justice for the poor, widows, and orphans. His Song of the Vineyard (Isaiah 5:1–7) illustrated how Israel, despite God's loving care and many blessings, committed acts of murder and injustice.

> Isaiah saw in Israel's great victories God's saving hand at work.

In his prophecies Isaiah recalled Israel's great moments, in which God's saving power was evident, in contrast to how faithless and fickle Israel of his time was. It was Isaiah's interpretation of Israel's sacred tradition that distinguished him from false prophets. Whereas false prophets assumed that Israel's past victories guaranteed the nation would continue to defeat her enemies, Isaiah saw in Israel's great victories God's saving hand at work. It was God who was powerful, not Israel. And if Israel despised God, then Israel ran the risk of becoming God's enemy.

In the Bible, we see that true prophets—like Isaiah—looked at Israel's history the way God looks at it. False prophets looked at Israel's history the way humans prefer to see it.

Needless to say, Isaiah was not popular in the king's court. On one occasion Isaiah approached King Ahaz to warn him against trusting in the Assyrians and their gods: "If you will not believe, surely you shall not be established" (Isaiah 7:9). In the original Hebrew there is a play on the words "believe" and "established." These words are two forms of the word *amen*, which means "believable," "trustworthy," "firm," or "established." This word is the key word in God's covenant with David: "And your house and your kingdom shall be established [*amen*]" (2 Samuel 7:16). Isaiah implied that if King Ahaz did not have faith in God, then he would jeopardize the promise God made to David long ago.

Isaiah was not the only prophet to remind Israel of her great promises, only to warn that Israel's sin will bring about judgment— promises or no promises. Jeremiah challenged the ruling priests who thought the presence of Solomon's famous temple in Jerusalem guaranteed the city's safety against the Babylonian threat (Jeremiah 7:4; 23:17). Ezekiel challenged the political elite who thought if Abraham, being only one man, could possess the Promised Land then surely a multitude of his descendants could possess it forever (Ezekiel 33:24–29).

The Need for a New Covenant

In 722 BC the Assyrian Empire destroyed the northern kingdom of Israel, also known as Samaria. The downward social and spiritual spiral continued until the southern kingdom, Judah, was destroyed by the Babylonians in 586 BC. The author of Chronicles summed up the demise of Israel this way:

> The LORD, the God of their fathers, sent persistently to them by his messengers, because he had compassion on his people and on his dwelling place. But they kept mocking the messengers of God, despising his words, and scoffing at his prophets, till the wrath of the LORD rose against his people, till there was no remedy. (2 Chronicles 36:15–16)

The kingdom of Israel was shattered. The temple Solomon had built lay in ruins, the people of Israel had been led away into exile, and the Davidic dynasty had apparently come to an end. But God was not finished with his people. The promises he made to Abraham long ago were still valid.

Israel had violated her covenant with God and because of this had lost her land, her city, her temple, and her kingship. But in time all of these things would be restored, because God is a merciful God. And in fact the restoration was not long in getting under way. In 458 BC Ezra led a group of Israelites back to Jerusalem. In 445 BC Nehemiah led more people back to Jerusalem. Under the leadership of these men the temple was rebuilt, new walls were raised, and the city of Jerusalem began to recapture some of its former glory.

But Israel still had no king. A new covenant was needed; and that was what the prophet Jeremiah promised:

> Behold, the days are coming, declares the LORD, when I will make a new covenant with the house of Israel and the house of Judah, not like the covenant which I made with their fathers. . . . This is the covenant that I will make with the house of Israel after those days, declares the LORD: I will put my law within them, and I will write it on their hearts. And I will be their God, and they shall be my people. (Jeremiah 31:31–33)

The new covenant would be realized through a new king—not another like the old kings of Israel, but a new king who will write his law on the hearts of his people. To this new king and his message and work we turn in the next chapter.

Summing Up and Looking Ahead

Throughout the Bible we see what happens to people who do not heed God's laws. These laws apply to all, including the rich and famous, the influential and powerful, as well as those of little means and no power. When people heed these laws, they fare well and society is much better. When people do not heed these laws, they fare poorly and society is much worse. Our modern society is no exception.

The teaching of the Bible, the "old book" that many people today ignore or think is no longer relevant, constitutes the very foundation of our civilization. The Bible has served us well; we ignore it at our peril.

At the center of the Bible is the most extraordinary person ever to walk upon this earth. His teachings permeate human society, especially in the West. Many of his parables and sayings are echoed in modern speech. He is the most influential person who has ever existed. His following is the largest of any following today or in human history. Many philosophies and religions seek his endorsement. More books have been written about him than about any other. Yet, curiously, many people do not know much about him. Many have not taken the time to read what his friends and contemporaries had to say about him. And many do not have a clear understanding of his teaching and his message. In the next chapter we will take a close look at this person—Jesus Christ.

Why Does This Matter to Me?

❀ Ignoring the teaching of the Bible—its commandments, its warnings—has dire consequences. The teaching of the Bible is for our benefit. Failure to heed it will at one point or another harm us. This is true for everyone, including you and me. Not even a king can escape the consequences of ignoring the teaching of the Bible. Why should I think I can?

❀ The law of God benefits all, especially the poor and the powerless. This should matter to anyone who cares about the weak and disadvantaged.

❀ The Bible provides a road map that shows us the way. We are foolish not to follow it.

7

Where Did Jesus Come From and What Did He Teach?

EVERY CHRISTMAS we celebrate the arrival of God's Son. One of the best-known Christmas carols captures the importance of his birth:

> Joy to the world, the Lord is come!
> Let earth receive her king.

The story of Jesus' birth is narrated by Matthew and Luke, whose respective Gospel accounts are blended together and presented as plays or pageants in churches every year. The world does indeed have a good reason to rejoice.

Many people know the Christmas story. But this story, as endearing as it is, doesn't tell us much about the world in which Jesus grew up. To understand well the teaching, proclamation, and activities of Jesus, it is important to know something about this world.

The world of Jesus was the world of early first-century Palestinian Judaism. The Jewish people were under Roman authority, either directly under a Roman governor (as in Judea and Samaria) or under the authority of Rome's Herodian puppet rulers (as in Galilee).

Almost always, misguided interpretations of Jesus do not adequately understand the context of Jesus. If this context is not understood well, then what Jesus taught, what he did, and how people reacted to him can easily be misunderstood. We must understand this context.

What did Jesus claim about himself? What did his earliest followers claim about him? To answer these questions we must address five important questions: (1) What was Jesus' relationship with the Judaism of his day? (2) What were Jesus' claims? (3) What were Jesus' actual aims? (4) Why did Jesus die? and (5) Why did the Church begin?

What Was Jesus' Relationship with the Judaism of His Day?

Through the centuries some people have viewed Jesus as opposed to Judaism in various ways. Christian theologians have assumed that Jesus criticized the religion of his people for being legalistic, for being caught up with externals, and for having little or no place for grace, mercy, and love. Jesus' action in the temple, traditionally referred to as the "cleansing of the temple" (Mark 11:15–18), was directed, we have been frequently told, against the system of sacrifice. Religion is supposed to be a matter of the heart, not rituals. Jesus understood this, but his Jewish peers did not. So goes this understanding.

Several scholars have rightly complained against this caricature. There is no evidence to suggest that Jesus opposed Judaism or criticized it as a religion of rituals. On the contrary, there is substantial evidence that Jesus accepted all the major tenets of the Jewish faith. These tenets include the unity and sovereignty of God, the value and sanctity of the temple of Jerusalem, the authority of the Jewish Scriptures, the election (or divine choice) of the people of Israel, and the hope of Israel's redemption.

Jesus also observed many of the practices associated with Jewish piety of his day: alms, prayer, and fasting (Matthew 6:1–18). Jesus fasted during his period of temptation (Mark 1:12–13); he prayed and taught his disciples to pray (Matthew 6:7–15; Luke 11:1–13; 22:39–46); he and his disciples gave alms, and he taught others to do likewise (Luke 11:41; 12:33; John 13:29). Jesus presupposed the validity of the temple, the sacrifices, and Israel's holy days (Matthew 5:23–24; Mark 14:14). He read and quoted from the Jewish Scriptures and regarded them as authoritative (Luke 4:16–22; 10:25–28; Mark 10:19; 12:24–34). Apparently he attended synagogue services regularly (Luke 4:16). His style and interpretation of Scripture reflect at many points the style and interpretation that emerged within the synagogue.

> There is no evidence to suggest that Jesus opposed Judaism.

Jesus also accepted the authority of Torah (the Law of Moses). He did not reject the Law, as some have asserted. What Jesus opposed were certain interpretations and applications of the Law. In the so-called antitheses of the Sermon on the Mount ("You have heard it said, but I say to you"—Matthew 5:21–48), Jesus does not contradict the commands of Moses; he challenges conventional interpretations and applications of those laws. For example, Jesus agrees that killing is wrong but adds that hatred is wrong too. He agrees that adultery is wrong but adds that lust is also sin. He agrees that swearing falsely is wrong but speaks against the practice of oath taking in his time. Jesus does not oppose *restitution* ("an eye for an eye"), but he does oppose using this command as pretext for *revenge*. He agrees that people should love their own people but adds that they should also love other people, even enemies.

Jesus seems to have believed that his own authority—which derived from the anointing of God's Spirit (Mark 1:10; Luke 4:18)—equaled that of the Torah. But his authority did not undermine the authority of the Law of Moses; it explained and applied it in new ways conditioned by Jesus' strong sense of the kingdom (rule) of God and the changes it would bring.

Jesus' innovative interpretation challenged conventional interpretations and applications of Israel's sacred tradition. In his Nazareth sermon (Luke 4:16–30) Jesus read Isaiah 61:1–2, a passage understood to promise blessing for Israel and judgment for Israel's enemies, and then appealed to the examples of Elijah and Elisha (Luke 4:25–27). From these examples, where these mighty figures of old ministered to Gentiles (1 Kings 17:1–16; 2 Kings 5:1–14), Jesus declared that his anointed task was to bless the marginalized, not only the righteous of Israel. This interpretation was daring—and was opposed by many teachers—but it presupposed the authority of Israel's Scriptures. Jesus' respect for Jewish Scripture places him squarely within first-century Judaism.

What Were Jesus' Claims?

What did Jesus claim about himself? This is referred to as the question of Jesus' self-understanding. Though Jesus says little about himself directly, there are many indicators that he understood himself as a special agent in God's service.

Jesus claimed to be a prophet. He said about himself, "A prophet is not without honor, except in his hometown" (Mark 6:4). The public also regarded him as a prophet, as seen in "A great prophet has arisen among us!" (Luke 7:16; see also Mark 8:28), and "If this man were a prophet . . ." (Luke 7:39). And, of course, Jesus made predictions (Mark 13:2) and uttered prophetic indictments against various persons, institutions, and groups (Mark 12:1–11; 14:58; Matthew 11:20–24 and Luke 10:13–1).

Jesus was frequently addressed as "rabbi" (Mark 9:5; 10:51; 11:21; 14:45). He taught as a rabbi, and his admirers said he taught as one having much greater authority than other teachers of his day (Mark 1:22, 27). Those outside his following addressed him as "rabbi" (sometimes translated "teacher" in Mark 5:35; 10:17; 12:14). Some scholars have asserted that the appearance of "rabbi" in the Gospels reflects an anachronistic usage of the title, since it did not become an official title until after AD 70. But the informal use of "rabbi" in the Gospels reflects Jewish usage in the first century, meaning "teacher," before its later, formalized usage.

Why would Christians writing after AD 70 apply a formal title to Jesus, a title used of religious teachers who were increasingly critical of Christianity? If anything, the title would have been avoided. That it is used so frequently suggests that the Gospel tradition is authentic. Jesus is called "rabbi" in the Gospels because, like it or not, he was addressed as such during his public ministry.

Although Jesus did not refer to himself as a priest, he performed some priestly functions. He declared persons "clean" (Mark 1:41; Matthew 11:5 and Luke 7:22) and "forgiven" (Mark 2:5; Luke 7:47–48). He also challenged temple policy and practice, put in place by the ruling priests. The most provocative challenge was the so-called cleansing of the temple (Matthew 21:12–17). In the later theology of the Church, Jesus' death and subsequent intercessory role in heaven came to be understood in sacrificial and priestly terms (as seen, for example, in the book of Hebrews).

Jesus regularly referred to himself as the "son of man," an epithet that has been debated for many years. In my judgment, this self-designation alludes to the "son of man" of Daniel 7. Jesus saw himself as this figure, to whom kingdom, power, and authority were to be given. This self-reference suggests that Jesus saw himself as God's vice-regent.

Did Jesus regard himself as the Messiah? It seems that he did. He was confessed as such by his disciples (Mark 8:29–30). When John the Baptist asked Jesus if he is "the one who is to come," Jesus gave a reply full of allusions to Isaiah 35:5–6 and 61:1–2 (Matthew 11:2–6 and Luke 7:18–23). It is clear that by this Jesus answered John in the affirmative. But did John ask Jesus if he was the *Messiah*? He probably did, judging by a recently published scroll from Qumran (4Q521). This scroll contains parallel allusions to the passages from Isaiah and understands them as the works of the Messiah. In other words, in his reply to the imprisoned John, Jesus implied yes, he is the Coming One (the Messiah), as is evidenced by the fact that he is busy doing the works of the Messiah.

> Did Jesus regard himself as the Messiah? It seems that he did.

Jesus' early followers viewed him as the Messiah. Shortly before his arrest, Jesus was anointed (Mark 14:3–9), likely a messianic anointing by a devoted follower. When asked by the high priest if he was the Messiah, Jesus said he was (Mark 14:61–62). And, very importantly, the Romans crucified Jesus as "king of the Jews" (Mark 15:26, 32). The charge "king of the Jews" only makes sense if Jesus had allowed his disciples and his enemies to think of him as Israel's Messiah.

Did Jesus regard himself as God's "Son"? The evidence here is tied to the question of Jesus' messianic self-understanding. David is called "son" in relation to God (2 Samuel 7:14; Psalm 2:7). The Messiah is therefore in some sense the "son of God." In 1 Chronicles 29:23 Solomon is said to have "sat on throne of the LORD"; so in a certain sense the son of David is expected to sit on the throne of God. This concept would add to the conviction that the Messiah would serve as God's vice-regent.

The most dramatic utterance, and one that ties together the Son of Man imagery with the Son of God identity, is found in Jesus' reply to Caiaphas. In an attempt to find incriminating evidence against Jesus, the high priest asks, "Are you the Christ, the son of the Blessed [God]?" Jesus answers, "I am; and you will see the Son of Man seated at the right hand of Power [God] coming with the clouds of heaven" (Mark 14:61–62).

To assert that Jesus did not regard himself as in some sense God's Son makes the historian wonder why others did. From the earliest time Christians regarded Jesus as the Son of God. Why not regard him as the great Prophet, if that is all that he had claimed or had accepted? Why not regard him as the great Teacher, if that had been all he had ever pretended to be? Earliest Christianity regarded Jesus as Messiah and as Son of God, because that is how his disciples understood him and how Jesus permitted them to understand him.

What Were Jesus' Aims?

The aims of Jesus are closely bound up with his proclamation of the kingdom (or rule) of God. Jesus proclaimed the kingdom of God and recommended changes of thinking and behavior in view of its appearance.

Jesus continued John the Baptist's call for repentance that was preparatory for the appearance of the kingdom (Mark 1:15; 6:12). Jesus believed his miracles were evidence of the kingdom (Luke 11:20). Jesus urged his followers to have faith in God and to forgive one another (Mark 11:22–25; Matthew 6:14–15). These urgings in themselves do not distinguish Jesus from Judaism, of course, but they take on a different nuance in light of Jesus' announcement of the kingdom.

Jesus promised his disciples that they would sit on thrones judging the twelve tribes of Israel (Matthew 19:28 and Luke 22:28–30). This saying gives us insight into Jesus' aims. He and his disciples expected to set up a new administration, in God's own time. This expectation coheres with the judgmental parable of the wicked vineyard tenants (Mark 12:1–11), which threatened Jerusalem's temple authorities with the loss of their position. The "vineyard" (Israel), will be "given to others" (to Jesus' disciples). This does not mean, contrary to some interpreters, that Gentiles or Christians replace the Jewish people. Such an interpretation is anachronistic and inaccurate. Jesus evidently expected his own disciples, at a time known only to God, to form a new government, to sit on thrones judging (in the sense of administrating, not in the sense of condemning) the twelve tribes. The reference to the "twelve tribes" also implies that Jesus fully expected the restoration of Israel—*all* Israel. This coheres with his call for repentance. If all Israel will repent, then all Israel will be restored.

One of the shocking and offensive features of Jesus' ministry was his association with "sinners"—that is, with people who did not observe the Torah (Matthew 9:10–13; Mark 2:15–17; Luke 15:1–2). Jesus taught that forgiveness could be readily and quickly extended to those who violated or neglected the Law of Moses. But this forgiveness required repentance and faith (Matthew 11:20–24; Matthew 12:39–42 and Luke 11:29–32; Luke 7:47–50; 13:1–5; 15:7).

Jesus' rejection led to a new element in his preaching and teaching. When he entered Jerusalem he was not greeted by the high priest (Mark 11:1–11). He criticized temple policy and practice (Mark 11:15–19). Ruling priests demanded to know by what authority he was doing these things (Mark 11:27–33). After his threatening parable of the wicked vineyard tenants, Jesus was challenged by various persons and religious parties (Mark 12:13–34). Jesus again went on the offensive, warning his disciples to beware the scribes who devour the estates of widows (Mark 12:38–40). Then, as a living illustration of this warning, he pointed to the widow, who gave her last penny to a wealthy and avaricious temple establishment (Mark 12:41–44).

When they left the temple, Jesus told his disciples that the buildings of the Temple Mount would be leveled (Mark 13:1–2). His aims of national repentance and restoration resisted, Jesus began to speak of coming judgment upon the city of Jerusalem and her world-famous temple (Luke 19:41–44; 21:20–24). It is in this context that Jesus uttered the words that were later used against him during his hearing before Caiaphas and the ruling council: "We heard him say, 'I will destroy this temple made with hands and in three days I shall build another not made by hands'" (Mark 14:58).

What Was the "Kingdom of God" for Jesus?

Though his birth is important, it is with his proclamation of the good news of the kingdom of God that the real story of Jesus begins to unfold. Mark boldly commences his Gospel account with the words, "The Good News about Jesus the Messiah, the Son of God" (Mark 1:1 ERV). These words echo the language of the Roman imperial cult of the divine emperor. According to the elites of Rome, Caesar is the "son of God" through whom the good news for the world begins. Mark says no to this claim and invites his readers to consider a very different Son of God, whose claim to such exalted status rests not upon his grasping for power but rather upon his astounding works of power and deeds of service. This is why we typically speak of the "ministry" of Jesus (instead of "career," for example), for the word *ministry* refers to service.

The ministry of Jesus was centered on his proclamation of the kingdom of God and manifested itself in five principal ways: (1) the proclamation of the good news, (2) healing and exorcism, (3) forgiveness and fellowship, (4) instruction in worship, and (5) service and sacrifice. Let's look at these five elements.

Proclamation of the Good News

Central to the ministry of Jesus was his proclamation of the good news of the reign of God, or the "kingdom of God." Mark tells us:

> Now after John was arrested, Jesus came into Galilee, preaching the gospel of God, and saying, "The time is fulfilled, and the kingship of God is at hand; repent, and believe in the gospel." (Mark 1:14–15)

During the course of his ministry Jesus sums up his activities with these words:

> The blind receive their sight and the lame walk, lepers are cleansed and the deaf hear, and the dead are raised up, and the poor have good news preached to them. (Matthew 11:5; compare Luke 7:22)

In Luke's version of the Nazareth sermon (Luke 4:16–30; compare Mark 6:1–6), Jesus declares that the words of Isaiah 61:1–2 are fulfilled in the ears of those in the synagogue:

> The Spirit of the Lord is upon me,
>   because he has anointed me
>   to proclaim good news to the poor.
> He has sent me to proclaim liberty to the captives
>   and recovering of sight to the blind,
>   to set at liberty those who are oppressed,
> to proclaim the year of the Lord's favor. (Luke 4:18–19)

It is clear that Jesus' proclamation of the kingship of God is indebted to the language and vision of the prophet Isaiah, especially as expressed in Isaiah 40:9; 52:7; 61:1–2. It is probable that Jesus' "good news" intentionally alludes to these passages that Isaiah proclaimed long ago. In all three of these passages Isaiah proclaims the presence and rule of God:

> Go on up to a high mountain,
>   O Zion, herald of good news;

lift up your voice with strength,
    O Jerusalem, herald of good news,
    lift it up, fear not;
say to the cities of Judah,
    "Behold your God!" (Isaiah 40:9)

How beautiful upon the mountains
    are the feet of him who brings good news,
who publishes peace, who brings good news of happiness,
    who publishes salvation,
    who says to Zion, "Your God reigns." (Isaiah 52:7)

The Spirit of the Lord GOD is upon me,
    because the LORD has anointed me
to bring good news to the poor;
    he has sent me to bind up the brokenhearted,
to proclaim liberty to the captives,
    and the opening of the prison to those who are bound;
to proclaim the year of the LORD's favor. (Isaiah 61:1–2)

In Isaiah 40:9 Jerusalem is portrayed as announcing good news to the land of Judah (the old southern kingdom). In Isaiah 52:7 we hear the good news that the messenger announces to Zion (or Jerusalem): "Your God reigns." In Isaiah 61:1–2 we are told of one who has been anointed to proclaim the good news of God's rule, a rule that will "bind up the brokenhearted," "proclaim liberty to the captives," and set free "those who are bound." The anointed messenger will "proclaim the year of the LORD's favor."

Jesus does all of these things in his ministry. He is the anointed one (Hebrew: Messiah). He sets people free from the bondage of sin and evil. His healing brings joy. Jesus confronts and defeats evil, and he gives up his own life to save his people. These prophecies from Isaiah clarify an important aspect of the meaning of Jesus' words, "the kingdom of God has come."

In the Aramaic translation and paraphrase of Israel's ancient Hebrew Scripture, Isaiah's words read, "The kingship of your God is revealed!" The verbal coherence is not to be missed: the good news of which Isaiah speaks is the announcement of the revelation of God's kingship. The most probable meaning of "kingship of God" is the "reign of God" or the powerful presence of God. This seems to be the underlying assumption in Jesus' rebuttal to the charge that his exorcisms were empowered by Satan rather than God:

> But if it is by the finger of God that I cast out demons, then
> the kingdom of God has come upon you. (Luke 11:20;
> compare Matthew 12:28)

The good news that Jesus proclaims is the in-breaking reign of God. God's powerful presence is at hand to redeem, save, and restore. Jesus' contemporaries would have understood his proclamation as the single most important part of his ministry. Isaiah not only defines the essence of the good news—that is, the revelation of God's reign—but the prophet also delineates several blessings of this reign, blessings that are witnessed in Jesus' ministry. To these blessings we now turn.

Healing and Exorcism

In the ancient world, ministry and healing were closely associated. Jesus' contemporaries would have viewed his healing and exorcism activities as important aspects of his ministry, so we speak of Jesus' "ministry of healing."

Thanks to the discovery of the Dead Sea Scrolls we now know that healing and proclaiming good news would have been viewed as evidence of the Messiah's presence. This is clearly seen in a scroll called the *Messianic Apocalypse*. The relevant part of this scroll reads as follows:

> The Lord seeks the pious and calls the righteous by name. Over the humble his spirit hovers, and he renews the faithful in his strength. For he will honor the pious upon the throne of the eternal kingship, setting prisoners free, opening the eyes of the blind, raising up those who are bowed down. And forever I shall hold fast to the hopeful and pious . . . and the Lord shall do glorious things which have not been done, just as he said. For he will heal the critically wounded, he shall revive the dead, he shall proclaim good news to the afflicted. (4Q521)[1]

This text echoes Isaiah 35:5 ("the eyes of the blind shall be opened"), Isaiah 61:1 ("anointed . . . to bring good news to the poor . . . proclaim liberty to captives . . . opening of the prison to those who are bound"), and Isaiah 26:19 ("your dead shall live; their bodies shall rise"). This vision anticipates a messiah who will heal, liberate the imprisoned, raise the dead, and proclaim good news to the afflicted. Jesus did all these things.

Interpreters have rightly observed that Jesus' deeds of power closely parallel the power of God, as poetically described in Psalm 107:

> Give thanks to the LORD, for he is good,
>   his love endures forever. . . .
>
> for he satisfies the thirsty
>   and fills the hungry with good things. . . .
>
> Some went out on the sea in ships;
>   they were merchants on the mighty waters.
> They saw the works of the LORD,
>   his wonderful deeds in the deep.
> For he spoke and stirred up a tempest
>   that lifted high the waves. . . .
> Then they cried out to the LORD in their trouble,
>   and he brought them out of their distress.
> He stilled the storm to a whisper;
>   the waves of the sea were hushed. . . .
> He turned the desert into pools of water
>   and the parched ground into flowing springs;
> there he brought the hungry to live. (Psalm 107:1, 9, 23–25, 28–29, 35–36 NIV)

Those familiar with the ministry of Jesus will recognize many parallels between the mighty deeds of God in Psalm 107 and the mighty deeds of Jesus recounted in the four New Testament Gospels.[2] Just as God calmed the sea, so did Jesus (Mark 4:35–41). Just as

God provided food in the wilderness, so did Jesus (Mark 6:30–44). Just as God healed his people, so did Jesus (Mark 7:31–37).

This is why Jesus closely identified himself with God. To see Jesus is to see God (John 12:45; 14:9; 18:6). Just as God is Israel's Shepherd (Psalm 23:1; Jeremiah 31:10; Ezekiel 34:15), so Jesus is Israel's Shepherd (John 10:11, 14; Hebrews 13:20; 1 Peter 2:25; 5:4; Revelation 7:17). Jesus must do the works of God who sent him (John 6:29; 9:4). Accordingly, Jesus can tell his critics that he and God the Father are "one" (John 10:30). Jesus is so closely linked with God the Father that he is empowered to forgive sin and in doing this restore fellowship.

Forgiveness and Fellowship

Jesus' healings were seen as evidence not only of the powerful presence of God, but as proof of his authority to forgive sins. The connection between healing and forgiveness is seen clearly in the story of the paralyzed man, let down through the roof by his friends (Mark 2:1–12). Impressed by their act of faith, Jesus says to the paralyzed man, "My son, your sins are forgiven" (Mark 2:5; see also Matthew 9:2; Luke 5:20). In response to the scribes who are offended by this assertion, Jesus heals the man "so that [they] may know that the Son of man has authority on earth to forgive sins" (Mark 2:10; compare Matthew 9:6; Luke 5:24).

Jesus' self-understanding as the "son of man" who has "authority on earth" derives from the vision of Daniel 7, where "one like a son of man" approaches the divine throne and receives "kingship and authority" (Daniel 7:13–14). This heaven-given authority empowers Jesus to proclaim the kingdom of God and to demonstrate its presence through healing.

Forgiveness is also linked to fellowship and the acceptance of the impure as pure. This aspect of Jesus' ministry is illustrated in the story of the woman who anointed Jesus' feet (Luke 7:36–50). Simon the Pharisee assumes that Jesus would not allow this woman to touch him if he knew what sort of woman she was (Luke 7:37, 39). Because he evidently does not know (so thinks Simon), Jesus must not be a true prophet. But Jesus turns the tables on Simon, challenging his assumptions. Jesus indeed does know the history of this woman, that she has been a sinner (7:47). However, her gratitude and extravagant love for Jesus, the proclaimer of the good news of God's mercy and forgiveness, provide dramatic evidence of her experience of grace. Before all, Jesus assures the weeping woman, "Your sins are forgiven" (7:48) and "Your faith has saved you; go in peace" (7:50).

> Jesus closely identified himself with God. To see Jesus is to see God.

Jesus reveals his insight into Simon's thinking by telling the parable of the two debtors:

> A certain moneylender had two debtors. One owed five hundred denarii, and the other fifty. When they could not pay, he forgave them both. Now which of them will love him more? (Luke 7:41–42)

Commentators have pointed out that the Aramaic word *hoba* means both "debt" and "sin," thus tying the parable to the issues of sin, forgiveness, and thanksgiving. Recognition of this nuance brings us back to the proclamation of the good news, especially in the tones of Isaiah 61:1–2, which is the "liberty" (or forgiveness) of prisoners and the oppressed. Jesus assures the woman that she has been released from the debts of her sin, which have burdened her and estranged her from the God of Israel. Recognizing this release, this forgiveness, she expresses her love and gratitude to Jesus. Her generous behavior contrasts that of the ungracious Simon.

Conservative, Torah-observant Jews, often identified in the Gospels as Pharisees and scribes, frequently objected to Jesus' intimate association with "sinners"—that is, with those who did not observe the laws of purity, as these critics understood them. This criticism leveled against Jesus is well attested in the Gospels. Let's consider an example. In Mark 2:15–17 we read:

> And as he reclined at table in his house, many tax collectors and sinners were reclining with Jesus and his disciples, for there were many who followed him. And the scribes of the Pharisees, when they saw that he was eating with sinners and tax collectors, said to his disciples, "Why does he eat with tax collectors and sinners?" And when Jesus heard it, he said to them, "Those who are well have no need of a physician, but those who are sick. I came not to call the righteous, but sinners."

The other side of the coin is expressed when Jesus remarks ironically, in reference to what his critics say of him:

> "Behold, a gluttonous man and a drunkard, a friend of tax collectors and sinners!" (Matthew 11:19 NASB; see also Luke 7:34)

The authenticity of this tradition can scarcely be doubted, for the early Christians can hardly have wished to characterize their Lord and Savior as a "friend "of hated tax collectors and despised sinners, reflecting not only dubiously on Jesus but also very poorly on themselves. No, this tradition, attested in our earliest Gospel sources, hearkens back to an important and controversial aspect of Jesus' ministry.

Jesus regarded the people to whom he ministered as "sinners" in need of redemption. He acknowledged that the sins of the woman who washed his feet "were many" (Luke 7:47) and that she was a "debtor." By characterizing himself as a physician ministering to the sick, and as one who came "not to call the righteous, but sinners" (Matthew 11:19), Jesus identifies those to whom he ministered and with whom he fellowshipped as sinners. On this question Jesus is in agreement with the scribes and Pharisees. The issue had to do with *what to do about the sinners*. Were they to be shunned and condemned, or were they to be ministered to? Herein lay a major difference between Jesus and many of the religious teachers of his time.

Jesus' outreach to sinners was not only consistent with his proclamation of good news, but it was the natural outworking of the good news. The rule of God was breaking into the world and changing the world. This meant liberty for captives, sight for the blind, forgiveness for sinners, and a new beginning for all. It also meant a new approach to worship.

Instruction in Worship

In the time of Jesus, issues of purity—of determining what was clean and what was not—were connected to worship. Only pure, unblemished gifts could be presented at the temple. In Mark 7 Jesus declares that the evil that proceeded from one's heart is what defiled a person, not unwashed hands or, by implication, other external forms of contagion. The parable of the Pharisee and the tax collector illustrates this point:

"Two men went up into the temple to pray, one a Pharisee and the other a tax collector. The Pharisee, standing by himself, prayed thus: 'God, I thank you that I am not like other men, extortioners, unjust, adulterers, or even like this tax collector. I fast twice a week, I give tithes of all that I get.' But the tax collector, standing far off, would not even lift up his eyes to heaven, but beat his breast, saying, 'God, be merciful to me a sinner!' I tell you, this man went down to his house justified, rather than the other. For every one who exalts himself will be humbled, but he who humbles himself will be exalted." (Luke 18:9–14)

This parable presupposes Deuteronomy 26, a passage that commands Israelites to bring their firstfruits and tithes to the temple and to declare that they are the children of Abraham and that they have obeyed God's law (Deuteronomy 26:3–10, 13–15). This is precisely what the Pharisee in the parable is doing. He thanks God for his privilege of being a member of God's chosen people (at the expense of various sinners and non-elect, such as the tax collector standing nearby) and declares that he has tithed faithfully.

The Pharisee's behavior corresponds to a description by the historian Josephus: "And when any man, after having done all this and having offered tithes of all, along with those for the Levites and for all the banquets, is about to depart to his own home, let him stand opposite the sacred precincts and render thanks to God, . . . Let him ask God ever to be favorable and merciful."[3] One also hears an echo of this Pharisee's self-righteous prayer in rabbinic literature: "I thank you, O Lord, my God, that you have assigned my portion with those who sit in the house of learning, and not with those who sit at street corners; for I am early to work on the words of Torah, and they are early to work on things of no importance. . . . I run towards the life of the Age to Come, and they run towards the pit of destruction."[4]

In sharp contrast to the Pharisee, however, the tax collector offers no gift and makes no self-assured statements about his covenant status. On the contrary, he confesses that he is a sinner and begs God to be merciful. According to rabbinic understanding, ill-gotten gains, such as profits from robbery and tax collection, could not be offered at the temple and disqualified a person from making the confession commanded in Deuteronomy 26.[5] The coherence between the details of Jesus' parable and this later rabbinic interpretation of Deuteronomy 26 confirms the realism of Jesus' parable and his insight into the religious thinking and practices of his time. The combined pronouncements of Mark 7 and Luke 18 teach that purity of heart and humility before God meet the test for purity and constitute true worship. Many of Jesus' Jewish contemporaries, of course, would have concurred.

Jesus teaches his disciples that if we are to worship God with a sincere heart we must be at peace with human beings. It does us no good to go to God asking for forgiveness when we ourselves refuse to forgive others. Jesus underscores this point in the Sermon on the Mount:

So if you are offering your gift at the altar and there re-member that your brother has something against you, leave your gift there before the altar and go. First be reconciled to your brother, and then come and offer your gift. (Matthew 5:23–24)

Jesus' famous Lord's Prayer also includes the injunction to for-give, even as we petition God to forgive us.

Father,
hallowed be your name,
your kingdom come.
Give us each day our daily bread.
Forgive us our sins,
　　for we also forgive everyone who sins against us.
And lead us not into temptation. (Luke 11:2–4 NIV)

Jesus' prayer is clearly an adaptation of the Jewish prayer known as the *Qaddish* (Aramaic, meaning "holy," "sanctified," or "hallowed"):

May His great name be glorified and hallowed in the world that He created according to His will.
May He establish His kingship in your lifetime and during your days.

Jesus took this common Jewish prayer, which he probably grew up praying, and expanded it to include petitions to God for daily needs, for forgiveness of sins, and for preservation from temptation.

If we are not willing to forgive sins, even as God has forgiven us, then we cannot properly worship God or fellowship with others.

Notice the reciprocity of this plea for forgiveness. Forgiving our neighbor correlates with God's forgiveness of us. Jesus emphasized this in his parable of the unforgiving servant. In this story, a man was forgiven a great debt but in turn refused to forgive a fellow servant a much smaller debt (Matthew 18:23–35). Jesus warns his disciples not to follow the poor example of the unforgiving servant.

Jesus' teaching on reciprocal forgiveness coheres closely with his teaching on love of God and love of neighbor: "You shall love the Lord your God with all your heart and with all your soul and with all your mind and with all your strength. . . . You shall love your neighbor as yourself" (Mark 12:30–31, quoting Deuteronomy 6:5 and Leviticus 19:18); as well as the Golden Rule: "So whatever you wish that people would do to you, do also to them, for this is the Law and the Prophets" (Matthew 7:12). We can hardly love our neighbor if we refuse to forgive him or her; and we surely would hope to be forgiven if we had caused offense.

> Forgiving our neighbor correlates with God's forgiveness of us.

Not only does Jesus teach his disciples to forgive, but he also teaches them what it means to serve and sacrifice. Once again, Jesus raises the bar to a new level.

Service and Sacrifice

Jesus' ministry is marked by startling teachings regarding service and sacrifice. Although not entirely unique, Jesus' exhortation that his disciples humble themselves and seek to serve is distinctive. Several sayings come to mind:

The greatest among you shall be your servant. Whoever exalts himself will be humbled, and whoever humbles himself will be exalted. (Matthew 23:11–12; see also Luke 14:11; 18:14)

If anyone would be first, he must be last of all and servant of all. (Mark 9:35)

Let the greatest among you become as the youngest, and the leader as one who serves. (Luke 22:26)

In contrast to the Gentiles who lord it over the weak and powerless, Jesus commands his disciples to think differently and to pursue a different course of action:

But it shall not be so among you. But whoever would be great among you must be your servant, and whoever would be first among you must be slave of all. (Mark 10:43–44)

We need to understand the stark contrast between servant and master in the Roman world. Slavery was common; citizenship was treasured. Military force was feared; political power was pursued. God's perspective, however, was very different. Jesus taught that greatness in God's kingdom is measured by serving others, not by acquiring wealth and power. According to Jesus:

Blessed are those servants whom the master finds awake when he comes. Truly, I say to you, he will dress himself for service and have them recline at table, and he will come and serve them. (Luke 12:37)

For who is greater, the one who is at the table or the one who serves? Is it not the one who is at the table? But I am among you as one who serves. (Luke 22:27 NIV)

In Jesus' world, a person who sat at the table and was served was regarded as "greater." But Jesus' values are quite different: he has come to serve, not to be served. From God's perspective, the "greater" is the one who serves.

Jesus demanded more of his followers than service only. He asked them to be prepared to suffer, even die, for his cause: "If any one would come after me, let him deny himself and take up his cross and follow me" (Mark 8:34). Although some critics suppose this saying arose in the post-Easter Church, there are good reasons for thinking it was uttered by Jesus. Jesus was fond of hyperbole (exaggeration that makes a point but is not meant to be taken literally); and suggesting that becoming his disciple was tantamount to taking up a cross and trudging to the place of execution was as hyperbolic as possible.

The expectation of martyrdom was consistent with Jesus' understanding of his mission, a mission clarified by the struggle envisioned in Daniel 7. Yes, thrones had been set up (Daniel 7:9), on which Jesus and his disciples would someday sit as they administered the tribes of Israel (Matthew 19:28 and Luke 22:28–30), but before this could take place a great ordeal would have to be endured. Satan and his allies will not go quietly.

Contrary to popular expectation and contrary to his disciples' wishes, Jesus anticipated his death. This anticipation led him to see another side of Daniel 7, for according to verse 14 all the nations were to serve the son of man. But according to Jesus, "the Son of man came not to be served but to serve, and to give his life as a ransom for many" (Mark 10:45 and Matthew 20:28). Here again Jesus believes that suffering must precede vindication and glorification.

The last part of this saying, "to give his life as a ransom for many," indicates that Jesus interpreted his death as substitutionary. This saying is consistent with Jesus' realistic assessment of the fate that awaited him. He had heard of what happened to John the Baptist. He was aware of the struggle depicted in Daniel 7. He had encountered stiff opposition from the ruling priests in Jerusalem. Had Jesus not reckoned seriously with the probability of being put to death, he would have been uncharacteristically naive.

Jesus would have been well acquainted with stories of martyred faithful, especially the story of the tortured and murdered seven brothers in 2 Maccabees 7. These brave lads believed that their fidelity to the Law and their willingness to die for it would bring reconciliation between God and the nation of Israel (2 Maccabees 7:33, 37–38). It is against such a backdrop that we should understand the words Jesus spoke at the Last Supper: "This is my blood of the covenant, which is poured out for many" (Mark 14:24). Jesus alludes to Exodus 24:8 ("Behold the blood of the covenant that the LORD has made with you"), Jeremiah 31:31 ("Behold, the days are coming . . . when I will make a new covenant with the house of Israel"), and Zechariah 9:11 ("because of the blood of my covenant with you, I will set your prisoners free").

But can we be more specific with respect to the factors that resulted in the death of Jesus? He himself found meaning in it and taught his disciples. But from the point of view of his enemies, why was it necessary for Jesus to die?

Why Did Jesus Die?

The most probable reason Jesus was put to death was that he made claims his opponents understood as messianic. The placard that the Romans placed over or near his cross, which read "Jesus, the King of the Jews" (Matthew 27:37), is the principal evidence for this view. There is other evidence Jesus held to messianic ideas, even if he did not assert his messiahship explicitly (which would have been inappropriate, according to Jewish expectations).

The Roman crucifixion of Jesus lends important support to the report that Jesus affirmed his messiahship in response to the high priest's question (Mark 14:61–64). Claiming to sit on the divine throne, *next to God himself*, would have been regarded as blasphemous and would have added incentive to hand Jesus over to the Romans.

Another reason Jesus' opponents sought his death was his threat against the temple establishment. In his parable of the wicked vineyard tenants, Jesus not only hinted that the ruling priests would lose their place, but he predicted that because of them the temple would be destroyed. That the ruling priests could be deeply offended by such rhetoric is illustrated in the experience of another man named Jesus, the son of Ananias, who some thirty years after the death of Jesus of Nazareth wandered around the city of Jerusalem, sometimes near the temple, uttering woes based on Jeremiah 7. (Jesus' criticism of temple polity also had been based on Jeremiah 7.) According to Josephus,[6] this man was seized by the ruling priests, who interrogated him and beat him, and then was handed over to the Roman governor with demands that he be put to death. The governor interrogated him further, beat him further, and decided to release him as a harmless lunatic.

Jesus of Nazareth was not crucified because he quarreled with Pharisees over matters of legal interpretation. He was not crucified because he taught love, mercy, and forgiveness. Jesus was not crucified because he associated with sinners. He was not crucified because he was a good man. Jesus was crucified because he threatened the political establishment with the prospects of undesired change. His contemporaries foresaw the possibility of a serious riot, perhaps even a full-scale rebellion.

The Jewish leaders (principally the high priest and the ruling priests) were responsible to the Roman governor to maintain law and order, and the governor was in turn answerable to Rome. Jesus was viewed as a troublemaker by these authorities, so he had to go. Because Jesus did not have armed followers, there was no need to seize any of his following. Hence, there was no battle or bloodshed beyond the crucifixion of Jesus himself. (That would change later, as the Church grew in numbers and the authorities attempted to destroy it. The persecution directed against the Church grew increasingly violent and resulted in imprisonment and martyrdom. But none of this was the direct result of actions taken by Jesus himself.)

> Jesus was crucified because he threatened the political establishment with the prospects of undesired change.

Jesus anticipated his death, found meaning in it, and urged his disciples to be prepared to follow his example. This was one part of Jesus' teaching that did not go over particularly well with his disciples. He had asked James and John, the sons of Zebedee, if they were prepared to drink the cup of suffering with him (Mark 10:38). James and John said they were willing to share Jesus' fate, but their actions later proved otherwise. When Jesus was arrested, his disciples fled; one of them betrayed him, while another denied knowing him.

But the lessons Jesus taught his disciples obviously did take root, for after the resurrection of Jesus they testified boldly to Jesus' messiahship, divinity, and resurrection, and founded a Church that within three centuries overwhelmed the Roman Empire. The young Church attempted to emulate Jesus' example and to implement his teaching. Jesus' openness to the marginalized paved the way for the Church's outreach to Gentiles and set the pattern that the Church has followed down through the centuries.

Why Did the Early Church Begin?

The early Church began because of its firm belief that Jesus had been raised from the dead and had appeared to dozens, even hundreds, of his followers. From its inception the early Church proclaimed the resurrection of Jesus. Apart from the resurrection there would be no reason for Jesus' followers to develop and maintain a distinctive identity. Jesus' teaching had not condemned Judaism, so there would have been little reason for his followers, most of whom were Jewish people, to abandon or modify aspects of Judaism, especially something as controversial as proselytizing non-Jews, without following the religious norms.

It was the unshakable conviction that God had raised Jesus that led to the emergence of the Church. The Church believed that its Lord and Savior would return. But what should believers do until he returned? How would the Church survive, especially in view of its growing estrangement from Judaism and increasing persecution at the hands of the pagan state? The writings of the New Testament were produced, in part, to answer these questions.

These writings continue to inform and inspire the followers of Jesus today. The Gospels tell the story of Jesus from different perspectives. As we have seen, Matthew writes so that Jews will understand how Jesus fulfilled the Law of Moses and fulfilled the messianic oracles of the prophets. Mark wrote to challenge the Roman Empire, guiding them away from the failed emperor cult to Jesus, the true Son of God. Luke wrote to show non-Jews that Jesus the Jewish Messiah was their Savior too. John wrote to show that Jesus was the embodiment of God's Word and Wisdom. Paul and other New Testament writers penned their letters to explain how the life, teaching, death, and resurrection of Jesus apply to our lives in transformational, redemptive ways.

> These writings continue to inform and inspire the followers of Jesus today.

The New Testament writings are almost two thousand years old, but they are not out of date. They continue to speak to human hearts, transforming and redeeming as effectively today as they did when they were first written. The redemptive, saving work of Jesus packs as much punch now as it did then. Two thousand years ago, the work of the resurrected Jesus transformed pagan Rome and Europe, leading the way to modern civilization on a level never before seen in human history. This resurrected Jesus can still transform us and our society if we let him.

Summing Up and Looking Ahead

Jesus' ministry was defined by the proclamation of the good news of the kingdom of God. The good news included the restoration and redemption of Israel, a new covenant, and the salvation of lost souls through Jesus' substitutionary death. The theme of freedom guided all other aspects of Jesus' ministry. The reality and power of the good news were demonstrated in healing and exorcism—the freeing of hostages, as it were, from the bondage of Satan and his allies. This freeing also entailed forgiveness of sin, which made fellowship with God possible. The freely bestowed forgiveness of God made possible, and indeed required, freely bestowed forgiveness of one human being for another. Such forgiveness then made it possible to worship God freely and humanely and made contemplation of personal sacrifice, suffering, and eventual death imaginable, even acceptable.

Jesus' ministry not only established the paradigm upon which the Church would be founded, it also put in place the principal components out of which Christian theology would be developed. Thus, Jesus' ministry should be regarded as an essential element of New Testament teaching and should not be pushed to the side (as is often done) to make room for the more systematic presentations found in the letters that his followers wrote. For Christians, Jesus' ministry remains normative for theology and teaching, as well as inspirational.

In the next chapter we will look at the ongoing significance of Jesus, asking why it is that his life, though lived long ago, remains of the utmost importance and relevance today. This question—What do I do with Jesus?—is the most important question you will ever ask.

Why Does This Matter to Me?

❋ The coming of Jesus was a game changer. Nothing was ever the same again. He fulfilled the Law and the Prophets and invited people to follow him. Jesus' invitation is still extended to each of us. Will you accept it? Why would you not?

❋ Jesus championed the cause of the powerless and the marginalized and faced down the powerful. How does that sound to you? At the end of the day, on whose side will you be?

❋ Jesus proclaimed the kingdom of God and demonstrated its life-changing presence with powerful deeds. For many this was good news indeed, but others responded differently. How will you respond?

8

Does It Matter That People Hear about Jesus?

RELIGIONS AND PHILOSOPHIES offer guidance for living. The resurrection of Jesus offers life itself. This is what makes it so important for you and me. What we will discover in this chapter is not just interesting, but it is life changing. It's the whole reason you're reading this book.

The Bible's account of Jesus' ministry with his disciples ends with his resurrection and ascension. The two events cannot be separated. The resurrection of Jesus inspired and energized his disciples. It confirmed his identity and the validity of his message. His ascension, on which occasion he charged his disciples with the Great Commission,[1] authorized them to continue his mission to seek out and save the lost, something his Church has been pursuing for two millennia.

Ten Reasons to Believe the Resurrection of Jesus

The resurrection is a certainty. In recent years some excellent books have ably defended the resurrection of Jesus of Nazareth. I list these books in the "For Further Reading" section. Here I want to share with you ten very good reasons for belief in the resurrection of

Jesus. Some of them are historical, scholarly, and logical. Others are personal.

Jesus Had an Extraordinary Ministry

Jesus was no ordinary teacher or rabbi; he was no ordinary prophet, no ordinary healer. Of him people exclaimed, "We never saw anything like this!" (Mark 2:12) and "He commands even the unclean spirits, and they obey him!" (Mark 1:27) and "He taught them as one who had authority, and not as the scribes" (Mark 1:22). When Jesus stilled the storm, his astonished disciples asked, "Who then is this, that even the wind and the sea obey him?" (Mark 4:41). Jesus was simply unparalleled. He so impressed his generation that professional healers and exorcists began invoking his name (Mark 9:38–40). Indeed, in the early centuries of the Church even pagans invoked the name of Jesus.[2] Even if they did not understand well who Jesus was and what he had accomplished, they knew that he was an extraordinary individual. Indeed he was; within three centuries his message swept the Roman Empire.

> Jesus' suffering and death did not take him by surprise; neither did his resurrection.

Jesus Foretold His Death and Resurrection

We can believe in the resurrection of Jesus for a second reason: he foretold it. "And he began to teach them that the Son of Man must suffer many things and be rejected by the elders and the chief priests and the scribes and be killed, and after three days rise again" (Mark 8:31). He prophesied this several times (Mark 9:31; 10:31–33). He agonized over it in the Garden of Gethsemane shortly before he was arrested. He asked that if possible, his Father might somehow make this suffering unnecessary. But if it was God's will, Jesus was willing (Mark 14:32–42, esp. 36). Jesus' suffering and death did not take him by surprise; neither did his resurrection after three days.

A Singular Resurrection Was Not Part of Jewish Belief

The resurrection of an individual was not what the Jewish people of this time anticipated. Sure, they believed in the general resurrection in the great Day of Judgment, when all will stand before God. But the resurrection of Jesus, of a single person? On the third day following his crucifixion? Literally? Unimaginable. In fact, when he first heard the prediction of suffering, death, and resurrection, Peter said, "God forbid, Lord! This shall never happen to you" (Matthew 16:22). When Jesus was arrested, all the disciples fled. Even Peter, who dared to enter the courtyard of the high priest where Jesus was being questioned and accused, denied knowing Jesus. When Jesus was led to Golgotha ("Place of the Skull"), the place where he was crucified, the disciples were nowhere to be found.

The Gospels Are Old and Reliable Sources

The four Gospels possess what historians and archaeologists call *verisimilitude*—that is, the Gospels exhibit the way things really were in their time. They speak of real places, real events, and real people. This is why historians and archaeologists make use of them. They know where to dig and they know what they have when they find it. Sources such as these, including the resurrection of Jesus, should be trusted. They were written at a time when the original followers and the people they taught were still living.

Women Were the First to See the Resurrected Jesus

The Gospels tell us that *women* were the first to visit the tomb and find it empty and then meet the risen Jesus. Fictional accounts would have told a very different story. In fact, we don't have to guess how fictional narratives would have told it; fictional narratives were written in the second and third centuries to respond to critics like Celsus and Porphyry. These men were skeptical because women (who in antiquity were not viewed as credible witnesses) were the first witnesses, while important people like Pilate, Roman authorities, and Jewish authorities were not witnesses. The *Gospel of Peter*, written in the second century, changes the story to reflect these criticisms. But the authentic, first-century Gospels did no such thing. They told the story as it happened. Women were in fact the first witnesses of the empty tomb and of the risen Jesus. The Gospels give us the unvarnished truth.

Followers Were Transformed

We can believe in the resurrection of Jesus because it is the only convincing explanation for the transformation of the frightened, discouraged, leaderless disciples into the bold apostles that they became. This was utterly unprecedented. Other charismatic leaders had come and gone, proclaiming things only eventually to be killed by the authorities. Their followers disappeared; their movements died. Not so in the case of the Jesus movement. Why was this? God raised him up, and his followers encountered him.

Skeptics Were Converted

The resurrection of Jesus is the only convincing explanation for the conversion of those who did not follow Jesus during his ministry.

For example, after the resurrection, Jesus' half brother James became the leader of the church in Jerusalem and later, like brother Jude, wrote a letter that is now part of the New Testament.

Enemies Were Converted

The resurrection of Jesus is also the only convincing explanation for the conversion of Paul of Tarsus, who violently opposed the church (Acts 9:1–22). In his letters Paul refers to his conversion and with shame recalls his persecution of the Church (1 Corinthians 15:9; Galatians 1:23; 1 Timothy 1:13). He did not believe in Jesus, did not believe that Jesus had been raised from the dead, and did not think Jesus' movement, the Church, had any validity. Indeed, Paul viewed the Jesus movement as a heresy that was subverting Jewish faith. Moreover, he had no personal ties to the Jesus movement. He was not related to Jesus' family or to any of Jesus' followers. In short, there was no emotional or psychological explanation for the man's change of mind. Yet while on a mission to stamp out the new movement, he completely changed. He went from persecutor of the Church to its enthusiastic supporter. What happened to this man? Paul himself supplies the answer: he met the risen Jesus. In his own words: "He who had set me apart before I was born, and had called me through his grace, was pleased to reveal his Son to me, in order that I might preach him among the Gentiles" (Galatians 1:15–16).

The Power of the Good News Is Transformational

The resurrection of Jesus is the only convincing explanation for the historical fact that everywhere the Christian faith goes and is embraced, culture is dramatically changed for the better. Christian faith has led to advances in science, medicine, education, art, music, the end of slavery, the promotion of human rights, and countless charities. Even the Chinese Communists recognize that what gave the West its edge was the Christian faith. Rodney Stark, distinguished professor of history at Baylor University, quotes a recent statement by one of China's leading scholars:

> One of the things we were asked to look into was what accounted for the success, in fact the pre-eminence of the West all over the world. . . . We studied everything we could from the historical, political, economic, and cultural perspective. . . . In the past twenty years, we have realized that the heart of your culture is your religion: Christianity. That is why the West is so powerful. The Christian moral foundation of social and cultural life was what made possible the emergence of capitalism and then the successful transition to democratic politics. We don't have any doubt about this.[3]

Jesus Is Still Changing Lives

Finally, we can believe in the resurrection of Jesus because the good news of the resurrection of Jesus still changes lives for the better. Countless people have stories of broken lives put back together. The positive impact of the good news is documented in much lower recidivism rates (that is, how many convicted felons reoffend and return to prison) for those who embrace the good news of Jesus.[4]

The transforming power of the good news of the risen Jesus motivates his followers to preach, teach, worship, fellowship, and engage in a variety of edifying and restorative ministries. The mission that Jesus launched did not end with his resurrection and ascension. It continues and remains as relevant today as the day it began. It is as relevant for you and me as it was for the followers of Jesus in the first century.

A Continuing Mission

The Church's mission was formally launched by the Great Commission, which is what we call the parting words of the risen Jesus to his awestruck disciples. In fact, this commission transformed his disciples from being learners (which is what the word "*disciple*" means) to being apostles or missionaries, words that derive from Greek and Latin, respectively, meaning "ones who have been sent." Jesus has sent his followers into the world to proclaim the good news. Here are the words Jesus spoke:

> All authority in heaven and on earth has been given to me. Go therefore and make disciples of all nations, baptizing them in the name of the Father and of the Son and of the Holy Spirit, teaching them to observe all that I have commanded you. And lo, I am with you always, to the end of the age. (Matthew 28:18–20)

Jesus' disciples are to make disciples of the nations, and to do that they are to baptize and teach. That is, the disciples are to share the good news of what God has done in his Son, Jesus, and then teach those who respond to the good news in faith. We call this task that Jesus assigned his followers "evangelism," which derives from the Greek word *euangelion*, meaning "good news" or (from Old English) "gospel." Evangelism entails sharing and proclaiming. It is not coercive or threatening. Those who respond to the message in faith form communities, or local churches, that are part of the universal Church.

The New Testament book of Acts chronicles the first generation of the Church, from its inception to the year AD 62. Acts focuses initially on Peter (chapters 1–12) and then focuses on Paul (chapters 13–28). It narrates the spread of the Christian movement from Jerusalem to Rome. One of the hallmarks of the new movement was its socialism (Acts 2–6). Early Christians who had surplus wealth gave to those who were poor (which the Jerusalem temple elite were not doing, even though the Law of Moses commanded it). The Church grew rapidly, despite serious opposition by the temple elite and eventually the Roman government. Acts concludes with Paul in Rome, detained, and awaiting a hearing before a Roman magistrate. Later Christian writers say Paul was released, which allowed him to travel as far west as Spain. He was rearrested and in AD 66 or 67 was executed. Even though the Christian movement was scarcely one generation old, it had spread throughout the Roman Empire.

> The Church grew rapidly, despite serious opposition by the temple elite and eventually the Roman government.

In AD 66 the high unemployment and indebtedness of thousands of Jews led to a riot in Jerusalem, which turned into a war for liberation from Roman control. The war ended in AD 70, with Roman troops battling their way into the temple precincts and torching the temple, something Jesus (and others) had predicted. With the city captured, Titus (emperor Vespasian's son, who commanded the army) looted and razed the temple. In AD 71 Vespasian and his sons Titus and Domitian held a great triumph in

Rome, celebrating the conquest of Jerusalem. Coins minted from the gold that had adorned the temple boasted the legend *Juda Capta* ("Judea captured") and depicted a Jewish woman kneeling before her Roman conqueror.[5]

Despite the intense persecution and martyrdom of the original apostles of Jesus, the Christian movement continued to expand and grow. Most pagans were polytheists and highly superstitious people; many were antagonistic toward Christians, calling for violent suppression of the movement. Nevertheless, the proclamation of the resurrection of Jesus and his message began to transform the Roman Empire. In just under three hundred years the Christian faith swept the empire. The spread of the faith involved no violence (no terrorism, no assassinations, no battles). Though martyred by the thousands, falsely imprisoned, and sometimes tortured, Christians attacked no one. Emperor Constantine himself was converted and in AD 313, in Milan, agreed that the Christian faith should be tolerated. Christianity did not become the official religion (as is sometimes claimed), but it was now legal, along with other religions.[6] Persecution of Christians came to an end. The Church continued to grow, advancing beyond the boundaries of the Roman Empire to extend to India and beyond in the east, on into Africa to the south, and up through Europe to the north and west.[7]

The New Testament's book of Acts provides readers with the first thirty years of the Church's life. We see how the new movement rapidly spread from Jerusalem, where it was first proclaimed on the Day of Pentecost, throughout Israel and Samaria, and on into the whole of the Roman Empire.

The Church was established in Rome long before Paul arrived.

We know this because Paul wrote his letter to the Roman Christians in AD 55. It was a church Paul was eager to visit. His letter to the Romans is considered one of the most important letters ever penned.

The establishment of the Church in Rome was strategic, for this guaranteed ongoing missionary work and communication throughout the Empire. Although at times severely persecuted, the movement that Jesus launched swept the Roman Empire in less than three centuries.

Summing Up and Looking Ahead

The Christian movement is centered on Jesus of Nazareth, primarily because of his resurrection. Had there been no resurrection, there would have been no movement, no preaching, and no evangelism. But the resurrection did indeed happen and because of it the Jesus movement was transformed. The timid disciples became fearless proclaimers. Because the Spirit of Jesus was present and active, the movement exhibited great power, a power that was perceived by sympathizers and skeptics alike. The result was rapid growth. In time the Christian movement crossed oceans and took root in faraway lands. The Church was no longer a localized entity but a worldwide movement, whose members swelled to hundreds of thousands and today number more than two billion.[8]

Does Jesus matter? Indeed He does. His ministry may have taken place two millennia ago, but it is a continuing, life-changing ministry that remains as relevant today as it was in the lifetimes of his original followers. His story is told in an old book, but it is the greatest story ever told, a story that is never out of date, never irrelevant. It is a story that becomes new every time it is told and—especially—every time someone embraces it.

The continuing relevance of Jesus helps answer the biggest questions that humans ask: Why are we here? What is the meaning of life? What is our destiny? Atheists have no meaningful answers to these important questions. They believe there is no purpose, no meaning, and—very importantly—no destiny. The atheist believes that the day will come when humankind will be extinct. It is a dismal perspective. But the Bible offers hope—not a pie-in-the-sky hope, but a real hope. The hope is real because of the person of Jesus of Nazareth, a real person who lived, died, and was raised up to new life.

The hope that Jesus brings has implications for the world's future and for our future as individuals. In the following chapter we shall look at what the Bible says about the future, or "end of the world," as some put it.

Why Does This Matter to Me?

* Belief in the resurrection of Jesus rests on much more than pious hope and naive credulity. It rests on well-documented eyewitness testimony and on the dramatic transformative power seen not only in the lives of the original followers of Jesus but in the lives of his followers down through the centuries. The reality of the resurrection matters hugely to every one of us, because the implications are quite personal.

* The resurrection of Jesus is not simply a philosophy or lifestyle. It changes everything. It means that death

has been defeated and that our earthly lives are not the sum total of our existence and what we are. The resurrection matters, because it confirms that there *is* life after death. What will you do to prepare for your eternity?

❀ Because of the resurrection of Jesus you and I have real hope. We can be sure that sickness and death will not in fact have the final word—for us or our loved ones. This is the good news that Jesus' followers have been proclaiming since the first Easter some two thousand years ago. It is indeed good news for each of us!

9

Why Do We Need to Hear about the End of the World?

TODAY THE NUMBER of Christians around the world is estimated to be about 2.2 billion, or just under one third of the human population.[1] This reminds us of what God promised Abraham some four thousand years ago: "Look toward heaven, and number the stars, if you are able to number them. So shall your offspring be" (Genesis 15:5). God promised Abraham land, posterity, and blessing. In one form or another every facet of this promise has been fulfilled, yet there is still more to come. The mission of the Church continues. The Great Commission remains in force.

In our contemporary Western society, we often hear voices calling for an end of faith in God and an end of trust in the Bible. But what happens when we turn our back on God and his promises? As our secular society distances itself from God and his story of love and transformation, we are seeing dreadful results. The West is in a state of moral and spiritual decline. Our youth are pessimistic about the future. Drug use, sexual abuse, abortions, suicide, and hopelessness have reached levels that have never been seen in modern Western society. Like many others of our generation, you may be asking, "What has gone wrong?"

I have no doubt that the problems we see today are the tragic result of the collapse of morality, which is the result of society's turning its back on God and what he teaches us, both in his creation and in his revelation found in the Bible. Our problems will not go away until we return to God and hear again his message. In today's world, the Bible has become a mysterious, unread book. It is time to change that.

Where We Are Headed

In the preceding chapters I have traced the beginnings and the ups and downs of God's people through history. But the Bible's message is not confined to the past; it speaks to the present and foretells things that lie ahead. The Bible's story of the past shows us who God is and who we are. The Bible has sometimes been compared to an owner's manual for humanity. The comparison is apt. But it is also moot for many, because they do not consult the manual.

What will be your present and future? What will be your ending? Many people do not want to face these questions. They go on through life as though these questions need not be asked, as though no ending will ever come. But endings do come for all of us. Of course, many people are interested in the question of "the end." A number of scenarios are entertained.

Many of the futuristic scenarios we see in popular culture (in books and movies) are bleak. Rather than envisioning a utopia, where all things are wonderful, many secular futurists envision a form of dystopia. In some of these scenarios the planet Earth is destroyed, making it necessary for a few survivors to find refuge somewhere else. In other scenarios the earth is overcome by alien beings, and humans are either exterminated or enslaved. In yet other scenarios humans somehow manage to survive, but life on earth is horrible.

Also bleak, but at least a bit more optimistic, are scenarios in which a threatened humanity is saved by a superhero. Dangerous villains are defeated by the Hulk or Spiderman or Thor or the like. Other heroes are far more ambiguous. What are we to make of the X-Men? According to this scenario humanity as we know it is rapidly becoming obsolete. New humans, given remarkable abilities thanks to genetic mutation, are on the rise. We old humans are now an endangered species, perhaps to be thrust aside in the not too distant future.

Perhaps less fantastic but almost as bleak are the worries concerning climate change. The science is much disputed, with some (usually astronomers) suggesting that the global warming of the last couple of decades of the twentieth century was due to an increase in the sun's temperature, and others (an assortment of scientists, celebrities, and politicians) warning that global warming and the resulting changes in climate are largely due to human activity. Whatever the true science happens to be, a lot of people are worried, forecasting grim scenarios of weather-related disasters, food shortages, political upheavals, and a general decline in the quality of life and security.

Lying behind a lot of these dark prognostications are fear and the almost complete absence of hope. This loss of faith in God undoubtedly has been a major factor in the doomsday crowd's pessimism and hopelessness. This pessimism in today's society, especially in the West, is also a major factor in the increasing levels of hopelessness and despair among high school and college students. Tragically, this sense of no hope sometimes leads to suicide and other forms of destructive behavior.[2]

In response, Christians, historically known as "people of the Book," remind today's frightened society that God is still sovereign and his redemptive work in his Son, Jesus, remains as relevant and effective as ever. Christians have every reason to continue proclaiming the good news of Jesus, even if it is not politically correct and in some settings is strongly discouraged, even prohibited. In Jesus the Messiah there is still hope.

> The Bible teaches that human life on this planet has a purpose.

But Christians are not always discerning in how they present their confidence and hope. Notwithstanding Jesus' own instruction that with respect to the Day of Judgment, "No one knows, not even the angels of heaven, nor the Son, but the Father only" (Matthew 24:36), some Christians claim to know the day that Jesus will return or the day the world will end. Only a few years ago a radio Bible teacher claimed that Jesus would snatch up Christians and initiate the final events of the end. This self-trained, self-published radio preacher proclaimed that Jesus would return May 21, 2011, and then after several months of catastrophes in which millions of humans would perish, the world would finally be destroyed on October 21, 2011. His prediction was based on a convoluted computation that no properly trained Bible scholar accepted. Of course, none of these prophecies came to pass. The radio preacher should have heeded Jesus' words.

As we have seen earlier in this book, the Bible's prophets were chiefly concerned with applying God's truth to their own times.

The prophets exhorted the wealthy and powerful and comforted the poor and downtrodden. The prophets called for justice and compassion. They spent very little time and energy thinking about the distant future and the day of final judgment. Concerning the end of the world, the Bible teaches that human life on this planet has a purpose. Our destiny is not left to chance. If we are wise we will place our trust and confidence in God.

What It All Means

I believe it is far better to ask life's big questions now and not later, and to seek the big answers while there is time. The Bible addresses and answers these big questions—all the questions that truly matter. Boiled down, the message of the Bible is not complicated; it is rather simple. The message of the Bible is that God created us and our world, and he did so beautifully. He draws us to himself through what we see all around us and in what he has revealed about himself in the pages of the Bible. But he has also given us freedom. God does not coerce. He loves us and wants what is best for us, but he doesn't force his love and will upon us. He wants us to love him back and to trust him, even when things go terribly wrong.

God promises us life, now and in the ages to come. In the work of his Son, Jesus the Messiah, we can have peace with God. God requires no mighty work on our part. We have no mountains to climb and no oceans to cross. God has already done the heavy lifting. He has sent his Son. What are we to do? In his great letter to the Christians in Rome Paul tells his readers:

If you confess with your mouth that Jesus is Lord and believe in your heart that God raised him from the dead, you will be saved. For with the heart one believes and is justified, and with the mouth one confesses and is saved. For the scripture says, "Everyone who believes in him will not be put to shame." For there is no distinction between Jew and Greek; for the same Lord is Lord of all, bestowing his riches on all who call on him. For, "every one who calls on the name of the Lord will be saved." (Romans 10:9–13)

Paul's statement is as simple as it is remarkable. Contrary to what most people in his day believed, the apostle asserts, "there is no distinction between Jew and Greek." For a man who in his previous religious life believed there was a deep divide between Jew and non-Jew, this is an astonishing statement. Paul was way ahead of his time. Today his sentiment has gained almost universal acceptance. Who today would say there is a distinction between one race and another? All of humanity was made in the image of God. There is only one God, and he is "Lord of all."

> We can let go of our follies and we can find new life. This is the message of the Bible.

Paul also says that all that is required of anyone is to confess Jesus as Lord and to believe that "God has raised him from the dead." If we do that, we are saved. Our end is settled; we no longer have to fear. God's gracious offer is not limited to the worthy or the righteous; it is open to every human being. Our loving and forgiving God "bestows his riches upon all who call upon him," not on those who deserve it or have earned it. Paul can say this from his own experience, when on the road to Damascus he encountered the resurrected Jesus (Acts 9). He can also say this because the prophet Joel said it too: "Everyone who calls on the name of the LORD will be saved" (Joel 2:32 NIV).

We can let go of our follies and we can find new life. This is the message of the Bible. It is a message that is well worth hearing and heeding. It is a message that continues to be relevant because human beings have not changed all that much. Our hopes and fears, our temptations and follies, are not much different from those of our ancestors. The good news of Jesus was sufficient for his generation; it is sufficient for ours.

Summing Up and Looking Ahead

In this chapter we have briefly reviewed some aspects of what is usually called "the end," whether the end of our lives or the end of humanity as a whole, or the end (or goal) of God's plans. Many in our world today are pessimistic about the future, including those who live in the prosperous West. Our society is fascinated with dystopic scenarios, in which the earth is laid waste or humans come to a violent and disturbing end, because our society has drifted from its historical biblical and Christian moorings. Because of this we have much fear and little hope.

Yet I believe we have good grounds for hope. This hope is not mere wishful thinking but is firmly grounded on what Jesus of Nazareth accomplished and on the continuing good news about him. In his redemptive work—his death and resurrection—we can have a meaningful hope. God does not ask us to earn our redemption; he offers it freely and graciously. All he asks us to do is to reach out and receive it.

In part 3 you will find four chapters. In the first one we consider how to find the Bible's meaning. Many people think the Bible is open to many interpretations and that its true meaning cannot be found. Is it really that hopeless? In another chapter we look at the violence and anger described in the Bible. Some people find this violence offensive and cite it as evidence of how out of date the Bible is. How should we understand this? We also examine the archaeological record, asking what evidence, if any, supports what the Bible says. You will find out there actually is great deal of solid evidence that supports the Bible. The last chapter puts everything into chronological order, so you will have a better idea of what happened and when.

Why Does This Matter to Me?

❀ Many secular futurists envision a dismal fate for humanity. But those of us who believe in God and heed his promises and assurances in the Bible envision an entirely different scenario. What scenario do you envision?

❀ Every one of us at one time or another wonders about the end—either our end as an individual or, perhaps, the end of humanity itself. Are you also concerned about this important question? We can find the answer in the resurrected Christ, the very center of the Bible's message. Have you found an answer?

Part Three

COMMON QUESTIONS
ABOUT THE BIBLE

10

How Do We Know
What the Bible Means?

WHENEVER WE READ a Bible passage, we want to know: What did the original author intend? What would his first readers and hearers have understood? What applications and further meanings does biblical text have? And most importantly, what does this passage mean to me—in my life, in my world—right now?

As we have seen, the goal of biblical interpretation is to discover as accurately as possible the original meaning of the text. This is called *exegesis*, from the Greek word that means to "lead out" of the text.

How we interpret a book of the Bible is also conditioned by the type of literature it is. The genres of biblical literature were discussed in detail in chapter 2. It is important to recognize a biblical book's genre because the genre has a direct bearing on our interpretive approach. Proverbs are not psalms and they are not prophecies. Not all prophecy is predictive. Parables are fictional stories, not news reports. We must also recognize other literary types, such as metaphor (figurative comparisons) and hyperbole (exaggeration), which should not be taken literally.

In this chapter you will learn five steps for how to interpret a passage in the Bible. In addition to these simple steps, you will learn further suggestions for studying the significance and meaning of Old Testament quotations and allusions in the New Testament. Finally, you will discover the importance of the Bible's background. If you are new to the process of biblical interpretation, I assure you: none of this is very complicated. In fact, you will find it very rewarding.

Interpreting the Bible, Step by Step

Step 1: Assess the Immediate Context

Bible professors often say something like this: "The three most important things in proper biblical interpretation are context, context, context." Context is absolutely essential, for without context virtually everything spoken or written will be misunderstood.

A classic example of a misunderstood Bible passage is found in a brief letter known as 1 John. In the middle of his argument John tells his readers, "you have no need that any one should teach you" (1 John 2:27). Without knowing the context, this assertion is counterintuitive, even contradictory. How can John *teach* his readers that they have no need for anyone to teach them? Why would any Christian leader tell fellow Christians there is no need to be taught?

I have encountered well-meaning but naive Christians who appeal to this verse as justification for not pursuing proper education. After all, they need no one to teach them, or so they think. Is this what 1 John 2:27 really means? Certainly not.

I did not quote the entire verse, nor did I say anything about its context. Quoting only a partial verse and not including the context account for the confusion about the meaning of the passage.

Let's look at the entire verse and the context in which it is found. To complete the sentence I need to quote verse 26 as well. Here are the verses in full:

> I write these things to you about those who are trying to deceive you. But the anointing that you received from him abides in you, and you have no need that anyone should teach you. But as his anointing teaches you about every-thing, and is true, and is no lie—just as it has taught you, abide in him. (1 John 2:26–27)

Verse 26 makes it clear that John is speaking of those who wish to deceive his readers. In verse 27 John reminds his readers that they have received an "anointing" of God's Holy Spirit. This anointing continues to abide in believers. It is this anointing that truly teaches God's people, and it "is no lie." Accordingly, God's people who are anointed by God's Spirit "abide in him."

We also observe that the verse is the conclusion of a unit of thought that began in verse 18, where readers are warned, "many antichrists have come." These antichrists are described as liars, in that they deny that Jesus is the Christ, or Messiah. The entire passage (vv. 18–27) is a warning directed against people who attempt to mislead the faithful.

What are "antichrists"? The word *christ* is a Greek word that means "anointed (one)." It is the Greek equivalent of the Hebrew word *meshiah*. It is from this word that we get the English word *Messiah*. The word *anti* means "against," "opposed," or "in place of." An "antichrist" is someone who opposes Christ.

These antichrists have abandoned the Christian congregation (vv. 18–19), to which the author of 1 John writes. Having abandoned the Church, they now deny that Jesus is the Messiah (v. 22). In this sense they truly *oppose* Christ. It is this false teaching, John explains, that his congregation does not need to hear. Some people who have left the Church (perhaps to return to the synagogue?) are teaching Christians that Jesus is not really the Messiah.

Once the context of the passage is understood, the assertion "you have no need that any one should teach you," now makes perfect sense. Hopefully you now see how important it is to consider carefully the context of any given verse or passage. You may find it helpful when these important steps are framed as questions: What paragraphs immediately precede and follow the passage I am studying? In what ways does the passage fit into the context?

Step 2: Assess the Broad Context

Another important aspect of context is what I call the "broad context." In the above step we considered the immediate context—that is, the verses that immediately precede and follow the verse or passage that is being studied. The next step concerns the broader context. Ask these questions: What is the thrust of the entire biblical book in which the passage occurs? Is this passage part of a larger theme or emphasis in the biblical book?

In our consideration of 1 John 2:18–27 above we focused on the immediate context of verse 27, which, among other things, tells readers that they "have no need that any one should teach" them. We observed that the "teachers" to be avoided are individuals who had left the Christian fellowship and now deny "that Jesus is the Christ" (v. 22). John calls them "antichrists," implying that they are persons who oppose the Christ (or Messiah).

What does the broader context of 1 John tell us? This letter begins in a way that is very different from most letters in antiquity:

> That which was from the beginning, which we have heard, which we have seen with our eyes, which we have looked upon and touched with our hands, concerning the word of life—the life was made manifest, and we have seen it, and testify to it, and proclaim to you the eternal life, which was with the Father and was made manifest to us—that which we have seen and heard we proclaim also to you, so that you may have fellowship with us; and indeed our fellowship is with the Father and with his Son Jesus Christ. (1 John 1:1–3)

The opening words, "which was from the beginning," are an allusion to the related work, the Gospel of John: "In the beginning was the Word" (John 1:1). The Gospel of John goes on to declare that "the Word became flesh and dwelt among us. . . . We have seen his glory" (John 1:14). When John speaks of what "we have heard," what "we have seen with our eyes," and what "we have looked upon and touched with our hands, concerning the word of life," he is emphasizing his direct and personal acquaintance with Jesus of Nazareth, the "word of life" (1 John 1:1), the Word that was "in the beginning," "with God" (John 1:1), and "became flesh" (John 1:14).

The point John is making is that he really knows what he is talking about. When he professes belief in Jesus as the Son of God and Messiah of Israel (John 20:30–31; 1 John 3:23; 4:14–15), he speaks from firsthand experience. He knows that the longed-for Messiah really has come. He saw Jesus' miracles (called "signs" in the Gospel of John). He also knows that not all Jews share this belief. In fact, Jewish leaders are driving out of the synagogue those who believe in Jesus (John 9:22; 12:42; 16:2).

This is the larger context in which we should interpret 1 John 2:18–27. The false teachers, called "antichrists," who should be ignored are those who oppose the Jewish Christians, arguing that the Messiah hasn't appeared, that Jesus is not the Messiah, and that Jesus isn't God's Son. Moreover, the antichrists viewed death of Jesus on the cross as proof that he was not the Messiah and Savior of the world. In this letter, John is responding to the antichrists' false teaching. Against this opposition he affirms that Jesus really is the Messiah and Son of God and that he came into the world to "take away our sin" (1 John 3:5). His death was not a setback or proof that he wasn't the Messiah; rather, it was "propitiation [payment] for our sins" (1 John 4:10). Jesus' mission was not a failure; it was a success.

I could say much more, but I hope this makes it clear how important context is for understanding the meaning of a given passage. The immediate context of 1 John 2:27 ("no need that any one should teach you") warns against false teachers, whereas the larger context of 1 John and the Gospel of John to which the letter refers helps us understand what the Jewish believers in Jesus faced in their time.

Having a fuller and more accurate understanding of context not only prevents arriving at a faulty interpretation, but it also brings the passage of Scripture to life. It makes its meaning more vivid and compelling. It often makes the passage more exciting too, as we catch a glimpse of the challenges the first Christians faced in a world that was often unfriendly and threatening.

Step 3: Consider Any Major Problems or Questions in Passage

After you study the context of the passage of Scripture, it is time to turn to the major problems and questions. Once again, it is helpful for you to ask a number of questions. These include: What literary form is the passage (or what forms are in the passage)? Are there difficult words, phrases, allusions, or Old Testament quotations that call for clarification? These questions are often solved through word studies and other comparative work. Yet more questions need to be asked: Are there textual problems (a verse missing in some manuscripts, or perhaps a different reading)? Are there some unusual parallels with other writings, inside or outside the Bible? Is there a historical event to which allusion is being made?

I realize that you might not be able to answer some of these questions. This is where commentaries on Scripture are especially helpful. If you are new to Bible study, you will find Tom Wright's "for everyone" commentaries easy to read.[1] Baker Book House's Understanding the Bible commentary series is a bit denser but not too difficult. You will also find very useful Gordon Fee and Douglas Stuart's *How to Read the Bible Book by Book*. This book, along with their *How to Read the Bible for All Its Worth*, will teach you what you need to know to begin reading and interpreting the Bible accurately.[2]

Let's return to our passage in 1 John. We have already looked at the meaning of the word "antichrist." But at this point we want to learn more about how Jews and Christians in the first century understood the meaning of *christ*. We have seen that basic meaning of the word is "anointed" and refers to the Messiah. But you might not know that in the time of Jesus, Jews held to different views of the Messiah. Some longed for a warrior Messiah who would conquer the Romans and drive Gentiles out of Israel. Others longed for a Messiah who would bring about religious reform and teach the Law of Moses with great insight and precision. Some imagined the Messiah to possess supernatural powers, while others thought of him in more human terms, as a sort of King David-plus. Given these kinds of expectations, we can understand why many in the synagogue near the end of the first century would be inclined to reject Jesus, a Messiah who died on a Roman cross and, apparently, had failed to deliver Israel.

Another word to study would be "propitiation" in 1 John 2:2 and 4:10. I mentioned that the word means *payment*, but there is a lot more to it. In the time of Jesus and earlier the word was used in reference to offering a sacrifice to God as payment, or "atonement," for sin, or for breaking the covenant. The word carried important sacrificial nuances in the Old Testament and in Jewish temple practices in later times. To understand well what the writer of 1 John meant it is important to study this word carefully.

Another important word to study is "abide," which appears in 1 John 2:19, 24, 27, 28, and elsewhere. It is important not only in 1 John but also in the Gospel of John. In fact, the word "abide" (Greek: *menein*) occurs forty times in John. Many of these occurrences are in teaching that Jesus gave in the Upper Room (John 14–15) the night he was betrayed and arrested. Abiding in Jesus is a very important theme in the Gospel of John and in 1 John. You are well advised to study this word and its several occurrences carefully in order to understand the point that is being made in 1 John 2.

Step 4: Interpret the Passage

After working through steps 1 through 3 you are now ready to interpret the passage. Here is the question you should ask: In light of the above research, what does the passage mean? In this step you bring together everything you have learned from studying the context and the major problems (important words, allusions to the Old Testament, etc.) you have encountered in your passage. Don't forget, in order to understand a given passage you must reconstruct as much as possible the world of thought in which the New Testament writer lived.

I should say a bit more about the importance of the Old Testament in interpreting the New Testament. Since the New Testament frequently refers to the Old Testament and presupposes its language, concepts, and theology, when you interpret a New Testament passage, you should be sensitive to the presence of the Old Testament and careful to reconstruct the theological context of a given Old Testament quotation or allusion. A comparative approach is essential. You must ask: How was the Old Testament passage quoted, alluded to, and understood by early Christians and Jews? To answer this question you should examine every occurrence of the passage, including the ancient versions and related literatures.

I know this sounds complicated. Again, this is where good commentaries can help you. If you really want to know what the biblical writer was saying and what his writing continues to say today, you do have to do some work. A good commentary will save

> In order to understand a given passage you must reconstruct as much as possible the world of thought in which the New Testament writer lived.

you a lot of trouble, in that it will provide you with information and insights that the commentator has assembled after years of education and careful study. The commentator is eager to share with you his or her insight. Don't pass up this opportunity. But you have to do some of the work yourself.

Step 5: Interpret the Whole Book

After you have carefully studied your passage, it is important to take one more step by asking this question: In view of what you have learned about the specific passage, what light does your new understanding shed on the biblical book as a whole?

Just as the biblical book as a whole provides valuable context for the passage you are studying, so the passage you are studying sheds light on the biblical book. There is reciprocity in biblical interpretation (and this applies to the interpretation of all literature). The whole clarifies the individual parts and the parts clarify the whole.

In the passage from 1 John 2 we noticed that by appealing to the whole letter, as well as to the Gospel of John, to which the letter makes reference, we understand our passage much better. Once we understood the passage, we saw it is an important part of the letter's argument and purpose. The author is dealing with the problem of people who have left the Church and are now siding with critics who deny the divinity and messiahship of Jesus and even go so far as to cast out of the synagogue those who confessed Jesus as God's Son and Israel's Messiah. Our passage in 1 John 2 is part of this larger controversy. Understanding more accurately what our passage truly means helps us understand better the larger message and meaning of both 1 John and the Gospel of John.

The Importance of the Old Testament in the New Testament

In step 4 above I underscored the importance of understanding how a given Old Testament passage was understood in the time of the New Testament. I should say a bit more about this important aspect of New Testament study (and again, you will want to make use of a good commentary such as the ones recommended in "For Further Study" in this book). To assess properly the function of Old Testament passages in the New Testament, you must consider the following questions.

What Old Testament Text Is Being Cited?

In the passage you are studying you might find two or more Old Testament passages combined, and each may contribute insight. Mark begins his gospel by saying he is quoting the prophet Isaiah, yet he quotes Malachi and then Isaiah, as though they are part of a single passage. Why has he done this? (Hint: Look for the word "way." Jewish interpreters in late antiquity often linked passages that had common words.) By combining passages from Malachi (which prophesies the coming of Elijah) and Isaiah (which prophesies the good news), Mark is able to link John the Baptist, who comes in the spirit and power of Elijah, with the good news that Jesus will proclaim. His linkage of the two prophecies is not haphazard but deliberate and insightful.

Which Text-Type Is Being Followed?

In the time of Jesus and the early Church, the Old Testament circulated in more than one Hebrew version and in more than one language, including Greek and Aramaic. Although these versions

191

and translations are quite close, there are interesting differences. As you interpret a passage, you will want to ask some important questions: What are the respective meanings of these versions? (Each may have an interpretive tradition of its own.) How does the version that the New Testament has followed contribute to the meaning of the quotation, and therefore to the meaning of the New Testament you are studying?

Obviously if you have not studied the biblical languages you cannot address this question. But it is worth mentioning here so you know that a New Testament writer may appeal to a particular version of the Old Testament because its language fits the context better or because the writer knows that it is likely the version most of his readers will know. Good commentaries will discuss the significant differences and help you understand various shades of meaning.

Is the Old Testament Quotation Part of a Wider Tradition in the Old Testament?

Every Old Testament quotation that appears in the New Testament is part of a larger passage of Old Testament Scripture. After all, every Old Testament verse has immediate and broad contexts. Accordingly, the New Testament writer may in fact have in mind the whole passage and not only the verse he has quoted. The Old Testament quotation that appears in the New Testament may be alluding to a context much wider than the specific passage from which it has been taken.

Sometimes a New Testament writer quotes only a small portion of a larger passage, which in turn may be one passage among many that treats an important theme (such as Israel's deliverance from slavery in Egypt or Israel's preservation in her wilderness wanderings). Remember, the Old Testament is not a book consisting of several thousand verses. It is a book consisting of long narratives, oracles, songs, and themes. The New Testament writers knew this, and sometimes they quoted one verse in order to bring to mind a major theme or a big story.

How Did Various Jewish and Christian Groups Understand the Passage?

When interpreting a biblical passage, you can gain a lot of insight by learning how the Old Testament was interpreted by various Jewish and Christian groups. For example, the Pharisees often disagreed with the Sadducees in their interpretation of the Old Testament. The men of Qumran (the collectors and writers of what we call the Dead Sea Scrolls) often disagree with the Pharisees and the Sadducees. Christian writers sometimes agreed with this group or that group and sometimes disagreed with all of them.

The New Testament itself provides information as to who interprets Scripture how. Josephus, the first-century Jewish historian, also helps. The Dead Sea Scrolls help us understand how Scripture was interpreted by the men of Qumran, while a number of nonbiblical writings from the first century BC and the first century AD give us a sense of the range of meaning in circulation in the time of Jesus and his followers.

Does the New Testament Citation Agree or Disagree with Interpretations in the Versions?

When you are studying an Old Testament quotation used in a New Testament passage, you will want to ask: Have Jesus and his followers given new meaning to the Old Testament text they are quoting, or have they adopted or endorsed meaning already in circulation?

In a number of cases Jesus appears to have given Scripture a distinctive interpretation, which his disciples use in their teaching. Jesus appeals to David's writing in Psalm 110:1—"The LORD says to my Lord: 'Sit at my right hand, until I make your enemies your footstool'"—in Mark 12:35–37 and then suggests that because David calls the Messiah (who descends from the line of David) "Lord," then the Messiah must be greater than his famous ancestor. That is, the Messiah is no mere "son of David," a David Jr., as it were. The Messiah is David's *Lord*. Accordingly, the Messiah is much greater than David. The followers of Jesus appeal often to this interpretation in their preaching and writing.

How Does the Quotation Contribute to the Argument of the New Testament Passage?

Finally, how does the Old Testament quote support the meaning of the New Testament passage? This last question speaks directly to the interpretive task. The reason we are studying the Old Testament passage that is quoted, paraphrased, or alluded to in a given New Testament passage is so that we are able to interpret more accurately the New Testament passage.

When you carefully consider these questions, your exegesis of the passage will be in large measure complete. Although the above steps have been applied to passages quoting or alluding to the Old Testament, you could use most of these steps for understanding and interpreting any passage, for it is indeed a rare passage that alludes to or parallels no other. Remember, what we call the "Old Testament" was all the Scripture there was in the time of Jesus and the first few years of the early Church. This Scripture was taken very seriously by Jesus and his disciples. We should take it seriously too.

Finally, I offer a few words about the importance of the background of the Bible.

The Background of the Bible

Christians regard the sixty-six books of the Bible as inspired and authoritative. As such, they are sufficient for faith and practice. However, by themselves these books are not sufficient for careful, thorough interpretation. That is because the books of the Bible were not written or read in a vacuum. Historical events, social customs, religious beliefs, figures of speech, turns of phrase, institutions, styles of dress, styles of building, and the lay of the land itself all contributed in various ways to what is said in the Bible and how its first readers would have understood it. These things make up what is termed the "background" of the Bible.

> This Scripture was taken very seriously by Jesus and his disciples. We should take it seriously too.

As time passed, readers of the Bible were less and less acquainted with these events, customs, beliefs, institutions, and geographical realities. Readers of the Bible filled in the details of the biblical stories with the details of their own lives, which often led to misunderstanding some of what the Bible's various writers were trying to say.

Bible background is the context presupposed by the Bible's writers and its first readers. How do we recover this context so that we can read the Bible today as its original readers did? We recover and reconstruct background of the Bible by taking into account several bodies of literature and fields of study.

Geography and Topography

Geography and topography refer to the location of places and the lay of the land in Bible times. Some of this is simple. For example, a visit to Israel, Greece, and Turkey (Asia Minor) will open our eyes to the landscape and terrain in which Jesus, the apostles, and the early church lived and ministered. When you visit these places—or even view the pictures in books or online—you can easily visualize biblical events such as Jesus' crossing the Sea of Galilee, with the crowds running along the shore, or going up a "mountain" (that is, a hill!), in order to teach the people.

Archaeology

Archaeology is the physical excavation and study of the past. As helpful as it is to visit the Holy Land, we cannot see things as they were two thousand years ago. Buildings have crumbled, streets have disappeared, and natural formations have changed. Archaeologists unearth these things and try to reconstruct them (sometimes literally, but usually only on paper), so we can have a more accurate idea of how they were. Thanks to the careful efforts of archaeologists, we now can see some of the stones of the temple and the temple mount, which Jesus and his disciples discussed (Mark 13:1–2).

Numismatics

Numismatics is the study of coins. Coins are often the propaganda of the ruling elite. They tell the public what they are supposed to believe. In Jesus' day, coins proclaimed the divinity and lordship of the Roman emperor or celebrated a recent triumph (such as the capture of Jerusalem in AD 70). The study of coins helps us understand better the point Jesus made when someone asked him about paying taxes to Caesar and he responded by asking to see a coin (Mark 12:13–17).

Epigraphy

Epigraphy refers to the study of what was inscribed on stone (or clay or metal). Inscriptions also played a public and often propagandistic function in society. Of course, inscriptions were often much longer and detailed than coin legends. The Priene inscription (located in southwest Turkey) celebrated the advent of Caesar Augustus, whose birth was regarded as the beginning of the "good news" for the world. This concept may well be important for understanding Mark 1:1, where the good news is said to have begun with Jesus. The Pilate inscription found at Caesarea Maritima clarified the governor's rank and public interests (Mark 15:1).

Papyrology

Papyrology is the study of papyri. Papyrus is ancient paper (the word *paper* comes from the word *papyrus*). Papyri provide us with personal letters, business records, deeds, lease agreements, reports, imperial decrees, and a host of other items. More than anything else, papyri give us glimpses into the routine of life in late antiquity. The letter of the prodigal son to his mother (first century AD) provides us with a real-life portrait of Jesus' parable of the prodigal son (Luke 15:11–32). The letter of Alexandros (third century BC) complaining of his servants being ejected from town adds a touch of color to Jesus' parable of the wicked vineyard tenants (Mark 12:1–12).

Comparative Literature

Comparative literature is the study of ancient writings that are not part of the Bible. This is probably the most important area of study in order to reconstruct the background of the Bible. More than anything else, the Bible contains ideas. Literature that parallels the Bible often helps us understand better the ideas of the Bible.

These writings are so numerous and come from so many different contexts and in so many different languages that few, if any, Bible scholars know all of them well. Some of this literature is "biblical," as in the case of the Old Testament Apocrypha, much of which is recognized as canonical by the Roman Catholic Church, the Greek Orthodox and Russian Orthodox Church, the Syrian (or Eastern) Church, and the Coptic Church. Other literature has a biblical flavor; much of this is usually classified as the Old Testament pseudepigrapha. (These writings are called *pseudepigraphal* because their authors claimed falsely to be famous Old Testament personalities.) Other comparative writings include the Dead Sea Scrolls, the writings of Philo and Josephus, rabbinic literature, various versions of the Bible, and the writings of the early church fathers.

Summing Up and Looking Ahead

Not everyone has the time to master everything discussed in this chapter. I hardly expect that. My point is simply to introduce you to the many facets of serious biblical interpretation. You don't have to be a scholar to get a lot of good out of the Bible. But if you aspire to be a scholar of the Bible, then you must do the things that have been briefly outlined here. If nothing else, I hope you will have a greater appreciation for scholars and clergy who spend a lifetime doing this hard work.

In the following chapter we will look at the expressions of anger and violence that appear in the Bible. How should these expressions be interpreted? Addressing this important question will give us the opportunity to put into practice some of the principles we have just considered.

Why Does This Matter to Me?

* Knowing how to interpret the Bible will enable you to discover what it really says and how it applies to you. Not knowing how to interpret the Bible is like wandering through an art gallery wearing blinders.

* Knowing how to interpret the Bible will protect you from being deluded by the quacks and the cults. It will also protect you from yourself!

* Of course, the greatest benefit from knowing how to interpret the Bible properly is that the Bible's many riches can become yours. What's stopping you?

11

How Should We Understand the Violence and Anger in the Bible?

PERHAPS YOU HAVE WONDERED, "What about all the violence and anger in the Bible? Doesn't all that bloodshed and fury just go to show that the Bible is completely outdated and no longer relevant in today's world, where we value freedom, peace, and acceptance of everyone?" I can understand why you would ask these questions, especially in light of so much violence in today's world that seems to be based on teaching in the Qur'an, the Muslims' holy book. Is the Bible like the Qur'an?

It must be admitted that the Bible does contain many stories of violence and battle. After all, it recounts the history of Israel, beginning with the nomadic Abraham and including Israel's conquest of the Promised Land, the many battles and wars to retain it, and its eventual defeat and exile. In addition to this violent history the Bible includes the writings of several prophets, many of which condemn Israel's enemies or Israel herself. If these violent elements are not properly understood, they could be taken as expressions of hatred. They could even be used to justify violence.

The Bible also contains many harsh utterances against various groups. The Jewish people, sometimes through their Old Testament prophets, rage against non-Jews and sometimes even against fellow Jews. Even in the New Testament we encounter Jewish Christians denouncing Jews who are not Christians, as well as Jewish Christians sharply criticizing Gentiles. Although much of the Bible is focused on grace, forgiveness, mercy, and love, there are admittedly some hard-hitting materials.

However, most interpreters properly understand how to interpret the angry and violent passages in the Bible. They recognize that much of the narrative material is descriptive. The battles between the Israelites and their enemies reflect the grim realities of life in antiquity and Israel's determination to secure its homeland. These battles are not templates on which we should today model our attitudes toward people outside the Church or outside our country. Such thinking would clearly fly in the face of Jesus' teaching, which instructs us to love our enemies and to pray for those who persecute us (Matthew 5:44).

Understanding the Social Context of the Bible

Not all readers of the Bible are sensitive to the various contexts in which things took place. Some read angry words of denunciation as timeless truths, applicable to any period. Many fail to understand the social context and instead read the biblical text through the lens of modern sensitivities.

In recent years it has become fashionable to assert that the New Testament contains anti-Semitic sentiments and bigotry. Those who claim this point to passages in the New Testament where one Jewish group or another is denounced. The problem with this thinking is that it tends to assume that first-century Christianity is basically Gentile and that the New Testament is largely a Gentile book, though perhaps dressed in Jewish garb. Seen in this light New Testament criticism of particular Jews and forms of Judaism appear anti-Judaic (opposed to Judaism as a religion), perhaps even anti-Semitic (opposed to the Jewish people).

Consider the bigoted tone the following passages would have if we (wrongly) assumed that the New Testament is a Gentile book expressing criticism of Jewish people:

> You brood of vipers! Who warned you to flee from the wrath to come? Bear fruit in keeping with repentance. And do not presume to say to yourselves, "We have Abraham as our father," for I tell you, God is able from these stones to raise up children for Abraham. Even now the axe is laid to the root of the trees. Every tree therefore that does not bear good fruit is cut down and thrown into the fire. (Matthew 3:7–10)

> Woe to you, scribes and Pharisees, hypocrites! For you build the tombs of the prophets and decorate the monuments of the righteous, saying, "If we had lived in the days of our fathers, we would not have taken part with them in shedding the blood of the prophets." Thus you witness against yourselves that you are sons of those who murdered the prophets. Fill up, then, the measure of your fathers. You serpents, you brood of vipers, how are you to escape being sentenced to hell? (Matthew 23:29–33)

Therefore I send you prophets and wise men and scribes, some of whom you will kill and crucify, and some of whom you will flog in your synagogues and persecute from town to town, so that on you may come all the righteous blood shed on earth, from the blood of righteous Abel to the blood of Zechariah the son of Barachiah, whom you murdered between the sanctuary and the altar. Truly, I say to you, all these things will come upon this generation. (Matthew 23:34–36)

O Jerusalem, Jerusalem, the city that kills the prophets and stones those who are sent to it! How often would I have gathered your children together as a hen gathers her brood under her wings, and you were not willing! See, your house is left to you desolate. (Matthew 23:37–38)

You are of your father the devil, and your will is to do your father's desires. He was a murderer from the beginning, and does not stand in the truth, because there is no truth in him. . . . Whoever is of God hears the words of God. The reason why you do not hear them is that you are not of God. (John 8:44, 47)

Are these passages anti-Semitic? Do they express contempt for the Jewish people? After surveying many of these passages and others like them the late Samuel Sandmel, a respected scholar of the Bible, concluded, "The New Testament is a repository for hostility to Jews and Judaism. Many, if perhaps even most, Christians are completely free of anti-Semitism, yet Christian Scripture is permeated by it."[1]

Some theologians and biblical scholars agree with Sandmel; others do not. Is the New Testament "permeated" by anti-Semitism? I do not think so. But how are the above passages to be understood?

In the first passage, the Jewish prophet John the Baptist rails against his own people. He warns them of complacency, of thinking that because they are descendants of the great patriarch Abraham they have nothing to fear. No matter what their sins—dishonesty, oppression of the poor, adultery, and the like—some Jews assumed that they would face no judgment. After all, Abraham was their father. John the Baptist, however, will have none of it. Mere physical descent from Abraham does not give one a pass.

But what about John the Baptist's rather colorful language? He calls those Jews he criticizes a "brood of vipers" (or "nest of snakes"). Is such language really necessary? Well, in John's place and time, it was necessary. His language is the very language of Israel's great prophets. For example, the prophet Isaiah angrily denounces his own people as "a people laden with iniquity, offspring of evildoers, children who deal corruptly" (Isaiah 1:4). He later addresses his people as "sons of the sorceress, offspring of the adulterer and a prostitute . . . offspring of deceit . . . who inflame yourselves among the oaks" (Isaiah 57:3–5 NASB). Jeremiah and Hosea liken Israel to a harlot (Jeremiah 3:6; Hosea 1:2).

John's harsh language brought to Jews' minds the harsh language of Israel's great prophets, those who long ago chastised Israel. These words may seem extreme, especially in today's society for which tolerance is the ultimate virtue. But the harsh words of the Jewish prophets long ago came to be cherished. Ancient Israel recognized them as words of discipline. The prophets of God rebuked the people of God because he loves them and desires them to change their ways. This applies to John too. His harsh denunciations were not expressions of hatred but words of chastisement, words intended to rebuke and bring about much needed repentance among his people.

The same applies in the case of the angry words of Jesus. He pronounces woe on the scribes and Pharisees, not because he hates them but because he wishes to warn them. Their hypocrisy does not accomplish God's will. Their legalism does nothing for the poor. If they and the ruling priests (whom Jesus also sharply criticizes in the temple precincts) do not change their ways, then all that they value—the temple, the sacrificial system, the city of Jerusalem itself—will be lost. John could see disaster coming; so could Jesus. And disaster did overtake the religious establishment in Jerusalem, when in AD 66 the poor and desperate revolted and ignited a war with Rome that resulted in the destruction of the temple and the deaths and enslavement of tens of thousands of Jews.

> The prophets of God rebuked the people of God because he loves them and desires them to change their ways.

What about the followers of Jesus? Paul visited Antioch of Asia Minor during his first missionary journey (Acts 13–14). After preaching the good news in the synagogue, he was reviled and contradicted. He then said, "It was necessary that the word of God should be spoken first to you. Since you thrust it from you, and judge yourselves unworthy of eternal life, behold, we turn to the Gentiles" (Acts 13:46–47). In saying this, Paul has not "written off" the Jewish people. He means that he now, in Antioch, preaches to the Gentiles. This becomes his pattern throughout his missionary travels: wherever Paul goes, he preaches first to the Jewish people, then he preaches to the Gentiles. This pattern matches his own statements in his letter to the Christians of Rome (Romans 1:16; 2:9). As the chosen people the Jews are given first opportunity. Only when they refuse does the apostle go to the Gentiles.

What about these words of Jesus? Has he "written off" the Jewish people?

> O Jerusalem, Jerusalem, the city that kills the prophets and stones those who are sent to it! How often would I have gathered your children together as a hen gathers her brood under her wings, and you were not willing! See, your house is left to you desolate. (Matthew 23:37–38)

Such language may strike us moderns as unfair generalizations, but again, this is the language of Israel's classic prophets. We hear similar generalizations in Jeremiah:

> From the day that your fathers came out of the land of Egypt to this day, I have persistently sent all my servants the prophets to them, day after day. Yet they did not listen to me or incline their ear, but stiffened their neck. They did worse than their fathers. (Jeremiah 7:25–26)

> For I solemnly warned your fathers when I brought them up out of the land of Egypt, warning them persistently, even to this day, saying, Obey my voice. Yet they did not obey or incline their ear, but everyone walked in the stubbornness of his evil heart. (Jeremiah 11:7–8)

The historian known as the Chronicler takes the same view of ancient Israel:

> Zedekiah . . . did what was evil in the sight of the LORD his God. . . . He stiffened his neck and hardened his heart against turning to the LORD, the God of Israel. All the officers of the priests and the people likewise were exceedingly unfaithful. . . .
>
> The LORD . . . sent persistently to them by his messengers . . . but they kept mocking the messengers of God, despising his words, and scoffing at his prophets, till the wrath of the LORD rose against his people, till there was no remedy. (2 Chronicles 36:11–16)

This summary reminds us of the words of Stephen, the first of Jesus' followers to suffer martyrdom:

> You stiff-necked people, uncircumcised in heart and ears, you always resist the Holy Spirit. As your fathers did, so do you. Which of the prophets did not your fathers persecute? And they killed those who announced beforehand the coming of the Righteous One, whom you have now betrayed and murdered, you who received the law as delivered by angels and did not keep it. (Acts 7:51–53)

This is no anti-Semitic rant; it is an example of the kind of prophetic criticism we find scattered throughout Israel's ancient and sacred Scriptures.

Understanding Other Jews During This Time

Jesus and his followers were not the only Jews at the turn of the era to say harsh things about the religious elites in Jerusalem; so did the men of Qumran, the men who wrote and collected the library we now call the Dead Sea Scrolls. Like Jesus and the writers of the New Testament, the people of Qumran quote, comment, and draw upon the Old Testament for their faith (who they are and what they believe) and for their polemic (where they disagree with others and on what basis).[2]

The author of the Hymns Scroll describes his enemies, the teachers and authorities of the Jerusalem establishment, in the following terms:

> They have plotted wickedness against me, so as to exchange Your law, which You spoke distinctly in my heart, for flattering words directed to Your people. They hold back the drink of knowledge from those who thirst, and for their thirst they give them vinegar to drink, that they might observe their error, behaving madly at their festivals and getting caught in their nets. But You, O God, reject every plan of Belial, and Your counsel alone shall stand, and the plan of Your heart shall remain for ever. They are pretenders; they hatch the plots of Belial, they seek You with a double heart, and are not founded in Your truth. A root producing poison and wormwood is in their scheming. (1QHa 12:11–15)[3]

Please understand that these angry words, written by Jews, are directed against fellow Jews. There is no racism here, and certainly no anti-Semitism. Another scroll speaks very harshly of the community's opponents. What I quote below is from the Rule of the Community, a scroll that lays out the rules for joining and maintaining membership in the "community" (Hebrew: *yahad*). Here is a description of those regarded as evil, including anticipation of their fate:

> The operations of the spirit of falsehood result in greed, neglect of righteous deeds, wickedness, lying, pride and haughtiness, cruel deceit and fraud, massive hypocrisy, a want of self-control and abundant foolishness, a zeal for arrogance, abominable deeds fashioned by whorish desire, lechery in its filthy manifestation, a reviling tongue, blind eyes, deaf ears, stiff neck, and hard heart—to the end of walking in all the ways of darkness and evil cunning. The judgment of all who walk in such ways will be multiple afflictions at the hand of all the angels of perdition, everlasting damnation in the wrath of God's furious vengeance, never-ending terror and reproach for all eternity, with a shameful extinction in the fire of Hell's outer darkness. (1QS 4:9–13)[4]

Many more passages could be cited. Elsewhere in the scrolls we find sharp disagreement with the Jerusalem high priest and his associates. The high priest is referred to as the "Wicked Priest" and other opponents of the Qumran community are variously called "Man of Lies" and "Preacher of Lies." The teachers of the religious establishment are called the "builders of the [whitewashed] wall"[5] (probably an allusion to Ezekiel 13:10–11).

In contrast to the Qumran's posture, the early Church proclaimed its message and invited all to join its fellowship. Never does the New Testament permit Christians to curse unbelievers or opponents. Never does the New Testament petition God to condemn the enemies of the Church. But Qumran did. If this group had survived, and had its membership gradually become Gentile over the centuries, and had its distinctive writings become the group's Bible (a hypothetical parallel to the development of the Church), I suspect that the scroll passages cited above would be viewed as expressions of anti-Semitism. But the Qumran community did not survive or become a Gentile religion. There is no subsequent history of the Qumran community to muddy the waters. So we interpret the Qumran scrolls as we should interpret them. We interpret them in their Jewish context, for they never existed in any other context and thus no one ever describes them as anti-Semitic.

This is how the writings of the New Testament should be read. And when the New Testament is read from this perspective, the assumption that it is anti-Semitic or anti-Judaic will rightly be abandoned.

Summing Up and Looking Ahead

Viewing the New Testament and the first two generations of early Christianity as anti-Semitic is hopelessly anachronistic. Early Christians did not view themselves as belonging to a religion that was distinct from Judaism. New Testament Christianity *was* Judaism—that is, what they believed to be the true expression of Judaism. Just as Pharisees, men of Qumran, Sadducees, and other teachers and groups believed that their respective visions of religious faith were the true expressions of what God promised Abraham and commanded Moses, so also early Christians believed that in Jesus God had fulfilled everything the prophets had predicted and all that Moses required. From a purely historical perspective, early Christianity was one Jewish sect among several.

To say that early Christianity opposed Judaism is to say that there was a clearly defined Judaism of the first century and that early Christians saw themselves as separate from it. Both assumptions are erroneous. Judaism was diverse and pluralistic, and early Christians viewed themselves as the righteous remnant within it (as suggested by passages such as Mark 4:11–12; Romans 9:27; 11:2–5). Just as the men of Qumran had done (1QS 9:18), Luke (probably a Gentile) calls Jesus' movement the "Way" (Acts 9:2; 19:23; 22:4; 24:14, 22). And like the men of Qumran, this self-designation may very well have been inspired by Isaiah 40:3: "Prepare the way of the LORD, make straight in the desert a highway for our God" (1QS 8:14; 9:19–20; compare Matthew 3:3; Mark 1:3; Luke 1:75; 3:4–6; John 1:23). This name provides one more indication that the early Christian movement saw itself as a movement within—and not opposed to—Israel. The New Testament writings reflect an in-house family dispute, not anti-Jewish feelings or anti-Semitism.

> Early Christians did not view themselves as belonging to a religion that was distinct from Judaism.

Historians and archaeologists find a great deal of useful information in the New Testament writings, especially the four Gospels and the book of Acts. In the next chapter we will look at some of the most important examples of this evidence.

Why Does This Matter to Me?

❋ Everyone who reads the Bible needs to interpret in context the stories that describe violence or the oracles and pronouncements that express anger. The stories are descriptive (not prescriptive) and the oracles are situational. It is important for us to understand that the violence and anger we find in the Bible do not authorize you and me to express violence and anger toward others.

❋ The anger expressed in the Bible almost always is intended to be restorative, to urge the wicked to repent. The anger is not destructive but redemptive. We should never use the Bible as a club, with which to beat someone over the head.

❋ Under no circumstances should the critical statements of Jesus or writers of the New Testament be understood as expressions of anti-Semitism. Jesus and his followers were Jewish; almost all of the writers of the New Testament were Jewish. The Jewish people are beloved of God. Anti-Semitism is ugly and it is very un-Christian. Anti-Semitism should have no place in your thinking or in mine.

12

What Discoveries Assure Us That the Bible Is True?

NAPOLEON BONAPARTE launched biblical archaeology when his forces invaded Egypt in 1798. Although they attempted to excavate, collect, record, and study materials, much of what took place was little more than looting. Proper archaeology began to be practiced near the end of the nineteenth century, and by the end of the twentieth century the discipline had become a science, thanks to well-honed methods and the help of new technologies.

In a column that appeared in a popular archaeology magazine, respected professor Ron Hendel provides a succinct definition of *biblical archaeology*: "Biblical archaeology involves the rigorous correlation of textual data from the Bible and material evidence from archaeology."[1] Very true. Archaeologists and historians find a great deal of correlation between the Bible and archaeology.

> Archaeologists and historians find a great deal of correlation between the Bible and archaeology.

Archaeologists are at work around the globe. In the land of the Bible (principally Israel, Egypt, Jordan, Greece, Turkey, Lebanon, Italy, and some of the islands in the Mediterranean) there are dozens of excavations under way in any given year. What archaeologists hope to recover are the remains of human material culture——pottery, coins, building foundations, mosaics, glasswear, tools, shoes, and clothing. In an ancient city's dump, archaeologists examine the animal bones to determine diet. These discoveries can tell us who lived in the city. (For example, in Jewish city dumps we almost never find pig bones, because Jews did not eat pork.) Coins and figurines tell us about political and religious ideas and affiliations. The quality of pottery and glass gives us some indication of affluence. Inscriptions are highly prized, because they provide us specific information, such as what language was used by the local population or by the elites.

Although the primary purpose of archaeology is to clarify the world of the Bible, its results often support the truthfulness of the Bible.[2] Below I provide a sampling of some of the most important archaeological finds, many of which support what the Bible says.

Relating to the Old Testament

The Rosetta Stone

During exploration and study in Egypt the French discovered a dark slate-colored stone near the town of Rashid (Rosetta) in 1799. We now know that it was inscribed in 196 BC on behalf of Ptolemy V. The inscription appears in three scripts: ancient Egyptian hieroglyphs (top), demotic (middle), and Greek (bottom).

After the British defeated the French, the Rosetta Stone, as it became known, came into the possession of the British in 1801 and was put on display in the British Museum, where it remains to this day. The text was translated (somewhat imperfectly) in 1803. The parallel demotic and Greek text enabled scholars to decipher for the first time Egyptian hieroglyphics. In reference to Ptolemy V, king of Egypt, the (Greek) inscription begins:

> In the reign of the young god, who has received the sovereignty from his father, the Lord of Crowns, who is exceedingly glorious, who has established Egypt firmly, who holds in reverence the gods, who has gained the mastery over his enemies, who has made the life of man to follow its normal course . . . the living image of Zeus, the son of Helios, Ptolemy, the ever living . . .[3]

Egyptian and Hittite Inscriptions That Mention the Habiru

During excavations in Egypt in the early twentieth century, archaeologists found inscriptions, some dating to the twelfth or thirteenth century BC, that mention a people called the *Habiru* who settled in Egypt. Scholars think this is a reference to the Hebrew people, who later become known as the Israelites. If this identification is correct, then we have extrabiblical evidence that supports the Bible's story of the Hebrew people entering Egypt and living there for a few centuries (Genesis 46–50). These inscriptions are housed in the Israel Museum and the Cairo Museum.[4] Hieroglyphic inscriptions that appear to mention the Hebrew people have also been found, dating to the thirteenth and fifteenth centuries BC.[5]

Sennacherib's Prism

Sennacherib reigned over the Assyrian Empire 704–681 BC. In the fourteenth year of King Hezekiah (probably 701 BC) Sennacherib invaded Judah and captured forty-six fortified cities and then besieged Jerusalem (2 Kings 18:13; Isaiah 36:1). Although the city of

Jerusalem was gripped with famine, and Hezekiah was powerless to drive off the Assyrians, Sennacherib abruptly ended the siege and returned home.

According to the Bible, Sennacherib was forced to withdraw because most of his army suddenly died (2 Kings 19:35–36; Isaiah 37:36–37). The account inscribed on Sennacherib's prism coheres with the biblical narrative at a number of points, even though there is no mention of the destruction of the Assyrian king's army. The prism reads:

> Hezekiah . . . had become afraid and had called upon the kings of Egypt. . . . I personally captured alive the Egyptian Charioteers with their princes. . . . As to Hezekiah the Jew he did not submit to my yoke, I laid siege to 46 of his strong cities, walled forts. . . . Himself I made a prisoner in Jerusalem, his royal residence, like a bird in a cage. I surrounded him with earthwork.[6]

All of this agrees with the Bible. What is strange is that the boasting Sennacherib does not explain why he abandoned his siege of Jerusalem. In his account he tells of killing or deposing princes and kings who had defied him. In Hezekiah's case, he is content to collect tribute, as he had previously. The biblical account seems to provide the explanation.[7] Sennacherib's Prism is housed in the Oriental Institute in Chicago, Illinois.

Tel Dan Inscription

During excavations at Tel Dan in northern Israel, two fragments of a stone inscription were discovered in 1993 and 1994. The inscription, dating to about 800 BC, describes conflict between Syria to the north and Israel to the south. In line 8 there is reference to the "king of Israel" and in line 9 there is reference to the "House of David." This is the oldest confirmed extrabiblical reference to Israel's famous king.[8] This inscription has seriously undermined the skepticism of so-called Minimalists, who assert that David is a fictional character. It is now widely acknowledged that David was a historical person and that he ruled over the kingdom of Israel.[9] The inscription is housed in the Israel Museum in Jerusalem.

Jerusalem Ruins from the Time of King David

In recent years archaeologist Eilat Mazar has been excavating in the oldest part of Jerusalem, just south of the Temple Mount. Her excavations have revealed a complex of buildings that may include a palace. Some of these ruins date to the tenth century BC, which means they may be the remains of buildings constructed by David and Solomon.[10] Mazar's excavations cohere with the Tel Dan inscription in that a complex of royal and administrative buildings is what one would expect to find if Jerusalem had at one time been the seat of an empire that reached as far north as Dan (just south of today's Lebanon border).

Qeiyafa Ostracon

While excavating at Qeiyafa, about twenty miles southwest from Jerusalem, archaeologists Yosef Garfinkel and Saar Ganor found in 2008 an ostracon, or piece of pottery, on which were inscribed five lines of paleo-Hebrew script. The text in places is not legible. It seems to be legislation concerning fair judgment relating to slaves, widows, orphans, and the poor. But that is disputed.[11] The importance of this tenth-century BC ostracon is that it attests a level of literacy in the time of King David that would be sufficient to record the narratives we find in the books of Samuel and Kings.

Even more importantly, the ostracon may be an announcement of the crowning of Saul, of the tribe of Benjamin, as Israel's king (1 Samuel 11:6–12:18). Saul may have been anointed king in response to the crisis brought on by Nahash the Ammonite, who had oppressed parts of Israel for some time (1 Samuel 11:1–5).

Relating to the New Testament

Pilate Stone

Roman historian Cornelius Tacitus (ca. AD 56–118), writing sometime around AD 110, referred to Nero's (ruled AD 54–68) brutal persecution of Christians, whom the maniacal emperor accused of setting fire to the city of Rome (in AD 64). Tacitus, known for his anti-Jewish and anti-Christian sentiments, mentions Jesus Christ: "Christus [Christ], the author of their [the Christians'] name, had suffered the death penalty during the reign of Tiberius, by sentence of the procurator Pontius Pilate."[12] Although Tacitus gave Pilate the rank of procurator, Roman historian A.H.M. Jones published a study in 1960 in which he argued that Pilate's rank was not procurator but prefect, as the Greek language in the New Testament Gospels seemed to imply. Jones's thesis received remarkable confirmation the following year when a stone was excavated at Caesarea Maritima, in which Pilate is referred to as "prefect of Judea."[13]

Inscription Relating to Grave Robbery

A Roman imperial inscription came to light in Nazareth in 1878 and was published in 1930.[14] The inscription contains a "decree" issued by Caesar, perhaps Claudius (ruled AD 41–54). Among other things, the decree forbids tampering with graves and the removal of corpses. The decree illustrates the seriousness with which people in late antiquity regarded burial and tombs.

The inscription reads in part:

> Ordinance of Caesar: It is my pleasure that graves and tombs . . . remain unmolested in perpetuity. But if any person lay information that another either has destroyed them, or in any other way has cast out the bodies which have been buried there, or with malicious deception has transferred them to other places . . . I command that a trial be instituted. . . . Let no one remove them for any reason.

This point stands in tension with those who think that the family and disciples of Jesus had little or no information about what happened to Jesus' body after his death or that members of his family would have attempted to remove his body from the tomb in which it had been placed.[15]

The Priests of Nazareth Inscription

Excavations at Caesarea Maritima uncovered in the vicinity of the ruins of a synagogue three fragments of a dark marble slab inscribed with Hebrew. Comparison with 1 Chronicles 24:7–19, which lists the twenty-four priestly courses, aids in restoring this formulaic and repetitive text. Fragment A has gained special attention owing to the probable appearance of the name of the town Nazareth in line 2. In line 4 of this fragment we are also able to restore [*m*]*gdl*, perhaps referring to Magdala, the hometown of Mary Magdalene. The

Priests of Nazareth inscription is significant because it provides archaeological evidence for the existence of a village called Nazareth.[16]

Caiaphas Ossuary

In November 1990, while working in Jerusalem's Peace Forest (North Talpiyot), which is 1.5 km south of the Old City, a crew inadvertently uncovered a crypt with four burial niches, in which twelve ossuaries (or bone boxes) were discovered. Happily, most of the ossuaries were found intact, unmolested by grave robbers. Coins and the style of writing on the inscriptions date these ossuaries to the first century AD. On one of the ornate ossuaries (ossuary no. 6, now on display in the Israel Museum in Jerusalem), two very interesting inscriptions were found.

On the backside and end of the ossuary the name "Joseph, son of Caiaphas" appears twice. Because Josephus refers to the high priest of the time of Jesus as "Joseph Caiaphas"[17] and "Joseph called Caiaphas,"[18] many archaeologists and scholars believe this ossuary once contained the remains of Caiaphas, the high priest who condemned Jesus and delivered him to the Roman governor (Matthew 26:3, 57; Luke 3:2; John 11:49; 18:13, 14, 24, 28; Acts 4:6).[19] The recent discovery and publication of an ossuary, on which is inscribed the words, "Mariam, a daughter of Yeshua, son of Caiaphas the priests of Ma'aziah," lends additional support to the identification.[20]

James Ossuary

On the backside of an ossuary the Aramaic names and words "Jacob [or James], son of Joseph, brother of Jesus" are clearly inscribed. Claims that the inscription is a forgery have been refuted, though the identification of the persons referenced on this ossuary is still very much an open question. Some think that James is none other than the brother of Jesus who was murdered in AD 62.[21] If so, his bones would have been placed in this ossuary in 63.[22]

Yehohanan Ossuary

In 1968 an ossuary was discovered at Giv'at ha-Mivtar, just north of the city limits of Jerusalem, containing the bones of a man crucified sometime in the 20s, during the administration of Pontius Pilate, governor of Judea and Samaria. This was one of the most dramatic discoveries in biblical archaeology. In the right heel bone (or *calcaneum*) was found an iron spike (11.5 cm in length) with wood fragments attached at both ends. To date, these are the only known remains of a person crucified in Roman Palestine. As such, this archaeo-logical evidence makes an important contribution to our under-standing of crucifixion. At the very least the Yehohanan discovery provides important evidence that Pontius Pilate in fact did allow for the proper burial, according to Jewish customs, of crucifixion victims.[23]

> Archaeological evidence makes an important contribution to our understanding of crucifixion.

The Shroud Tomb

In 2000 archaeologist Shimon Gibson and a number of his students discovered a recently vandalized tomb in Akeldama, in the lower part of the Hinnom Valley, at the foot of Mount Zion in Jerusalem. Although most of the ossuaries had been damaged and skeletal remains tossed about, an undisturbed corpse wrapped in a burial shroud was found in a niche. Gibson and fellow archaeologist

Boaz Zissu quickly excavated the tomb. Of special interest was the enshrouded corpse. Remarkably, some of the corpse's soft tissue, including hair and scalp, was still intact. Analysis of this tissue demonstrated that the enshrouded corpse belonged to a man who was related to most of the other occupants of the tomb. Analysis of the tissue also discovered the presence of leprosy, or Hansen's disease, thus confirming—contrary to the claims of some—that this dreaded disease did in fact exist in Palestine in the time of Jesus.[24]

Tomb with Round Stone

Although most first-century Jewish tombs were sealed with square block stones, some were sealed with round, wheel-shaped stones. The story of Jesus' burial and the discovery of the stone of his tomb being "rolled" aside (Matthew 27:60; 28:2; Mark 15:46; 16:4; Luke 24:2) imply that the entrance to Jesus' tomb may well have been sealed by a round stone.

Galilean Synagogues

Thirty years ago a skeptic suggested that there were no synagogue buildings in the time of Jesus. He argued that the New Testament Gospels and Acts, along with the Jewish historian Josephus, are anachronistic in speaking of synagogues because synagogues were not built until after AD 70, when the Jerusalem temple was destroyed. Virtually no scholar agrees with him, archaeologists least of all, for at least seven synagogues dating to the time of Jesus and earlier have been excavated. There are two other possible synagogues from this period of time, as well as two inscriptions that date to the first century AD. (One of the inscriptions bears the date December 3, 55.) The seven confirmed synagogues have been found at Gamla, the Herodium, Jericho, Magdala, Masada, Modi'in, and Qiryat Sefer. The two possibilities are at Capernaum and Shuafat.

The Gamla synagogue is located in the Golan Heights. It was destroyed by the Romans in AD 67 and was excavated in the 1970s. Gamla (Aramaic: "camel") gets its name from the camel-shaped spur on which the city is situated.

Although the beautiful limestone synagogue at Capernaum dates to the fourth century AD, the black basalt foundation beneath it may have been the foundation of the older synagogue that stood in the time of Jesus.

Of great excitement was the 2009 discovery of the synagogue at ancient Magdala, the hometown of Mary Magdalene. Given Mary's association with Jesus, it is quite likely that on at least one occasion Jesus preached in this synagogue. Magdala (Hebrew name: Migdal) overlooks the Sea of Galilee and is a few miles southwest of Capernaum.[25] The synagogue was constructed in the 20s, expanded in the 40s, and destroyed by General Titus in AD 67.

Found in the center of the Magdala synagogue was a decorated stone. Archaeologists think this distinctive stone, adorned with the menorah and other symbols that probably reflect temple themes, may have been used as a base for a reading table that would support Bible scrolls for reading in the synagogue.

Theodotos Synagogue Inscription

In addition to the substantial evidence of ancient synagogues in Galilee, we have evidence of at least one synagogue in Jerusalem while the city's famous temple was still standing. In 1913 archaeologist Raimund Weill discovered a stone slab on which were inscribed words thanking one Theodotos, son of Vettenus, priest and synagogue ruler, for building the synagogue and guest room. The slab was discovered among debris from the destruction of Jerusalem in AD 70, so it seems likely that this inscription and the synagogue to which it refers existed prior to the Roman destruction of the city. Moreover, the style of writing matches what we find in the Herodian period. Archaeologists and epigraphers (experts on inscriptions) date the slab to the beginning of the first century AD, perhaps even as early as the end of the first century BC.

The Jesus Boat

In 1986 two brothers wading along the shore of the Sea of Galilee, whose water level was unusually low, came across an ancient boat submerged in the mud. With great skill and ingenuity Shelley Wachsmann, professor of biblical archaeology in the Nautical Archaeology Program at Texas A&M University, and his team extracted, cleaned, and preserved the boat. Some think that the boat was used for fishing. Others suggest the boat was used for transportation and ferrying goods across the lake. In any event, the boat was retired and allowed to sink probably sometime at the turn of the era.[26] Although popularly called the "Jesus boat," the recovered boat in all likelihood had been out of service for a number of years before Jesus began his public activities. The boat is housed in the Yigal Alon Museum in Kibbutz Ginosar, Galilee.

Gallio Inscription

According to Acts 18:5–11 the apostle Paul spent eighteen months in the city of Corinth (in Greece). At some point during this time Paul was accused of inciting people to worship God contrary to custom and was brought before Gallio, the proconsul of Greece (also called Achaia). Lucius Junius Gallio was the brother of the well-known stoic philosopher Seneca. It can be inferred from an inscription found in Delphi (also in Greece) that Gallio was appointed proconsul of Greece in the year AD 51. This discovery helps us date Paul's time in Greece and again underscores the historical accuracy of the book of Acts.

The Palatine Graffito

The well-known Palatine Graffito was etched on a plastered wall in what is believed to have been slaves' quarters on the Palatine Hill in Rome. Found in 1857, the graffito dates to the third century, though it may reach back to the late second century. It is now housed in the Palatine Museum in Rome. The graffito depicts a crucified figure with the head of a donkey. To the left is another figure with upraised arm. This figure seems to be saluting the crucifixion victim and perhaps is blowing him a kiss. Between and beneath the two figures, written in four lines, are the words, "Alexamenos worships [his] god." The graffito is intended as an insult, both to Alexamenos as well as to Jesus. The donkey's head may have been a pagan insult of the Jewish people, suggesting that Jews do not depict their God because they are ashamed of what he really is and what he looks like. If this is true, then it is interesting that the Jesus movement, even at the end of the second century, remains closely linked to the Jewish people. The graffito is also important because it supports the traditional shape of the cross.[27]

Temple Warning

In 1871 Charles Clermont-Ganneau found a limestone block with an inscription warning Gentiles to stay out of the perimeter surrounding the sanctuary. A fragment of a second inscription was found in 1935 outside the wall around Jerusalem's Old City. Apparently there were several of these warnings posted in the temple precincts. Josephus refers to them as follows: "Upon [the partition wall of the temple court] stood pillars, at equal distances from one another, declaring the law of purity, some in Greek, and some in Roman letters, that 'no foreigner should go within that holy place."[28] The inscribed stone that Clermont-Ganneau found reads as follows:

> Let no Gentile enter
> within the partition and barrier
> surrounding the temple; whosoever
> is caught shall be responsible
> for his subsequent
> death.

Relating to Both the Old and the New Testaments

Nash Papyrus

In 1898 W. L. Nash acquired four fragments of papyrus from Egypt. Nash gave the papyrus fragments to Cambridge University. The Nash Papyrus was originally dated to the second century AD, but subsequent analysis has dated it to at least as early as the second century BC, which made it the oldest text of the Old Testament until the discovery of the Dead Sea Scrolls. The twenty-line Nash Papyrus consists of the Ten Commandments and most of the Shema (the well-known Jewish prayer that begins, "Hear, O Israel! The LORD is our God! The LORD is one" [Deuteronomy 6:4 NASB]). Jewish custom was to repeat the Ten Commandments and then say the

Shema. The Nash Papyrus probably represents a leaf of an ancient Jewish prayer book.[29]

Dead Sea Scrolls

From 1947 to 1956 over nine hundred scrolls were recovered from eleven caves in the vicinity of Wadi Qumran on the northwest shore of the Dead Sea. Of these some 220 are Bible scrolls (books of the Old Testament), while the remainder are commentaries on the Bible, prophecies, rulebooks, apocryphal materials, calendars, phylacteries, and other types of text and materials.[30] So far as the Bible scrolls are concerned, arguably the best known and most important is the Great Isaiah Scroll. Virtually the entirety of Isaiah's text is preserved in this ancient scroll, dating to about 150 BC (though some think it might reach back to 200 BC).

Summing Up

More than two dozen examples of archaeological evidence that supports the Bible have been given in this chapter. Dozens more examples could be provided. The correlation between the Bible and the artifacts and evidences unearthed by archaeologists and historians convinces scholars that the biblical writers spoke truthfully. If the biblical narratives were nothing more than fables and fictions there would be no correlation and no verisimilitude. Archaeologists and historians would have to study other writings, not the writings of the Bible.

The early Church believed that in the sacred writings, which today we call the Bible, God speaks, and the duty of the believer was to listen carefully that he might discern what is said and what it means.

Christians today believe that God continues to speak through these sacred writings. In today's discordant world, a world that has lost its way, what God is saying needs to be heard. It's hard to imagine a greater need and a greater urgency.

Why Does This Matter to Me?

* When considering big truth claims, most people want solid evidence. This is very true with respect to the Bible. It purports to be the Word of God, to narrate a history in which God was active among humans. There is a lot of evidence to support this. Knowing this evidence is important to confirm and support our faith in the God of the Bible.

* The evidence that we have is plentiful, and new discoveries continue to be made. These discoveries increase our confidence in the reliability and truthfulness of the Bible.

* Given the many confirmations that archaeology and history have provided the Bible, shouldn't we take its message seriously?

13

Who Did What and When Did It Happen?

STUDENTS OFTEN GROAN when told they are expected to memorize a few dates for an exam. "Do I really need to know this?" they ask. "Yes," I tell them, "you really do." Key dates are important, for the events of history are connected by dates. If we are to understand history, then we must first understand its chronological sequence.

The timeline below not only provides the important dates that pertain to the Bible, but it also provides many other dates. My hope is that as you learn more about the Bible and its history you will come to appreciate all the dates and events.

I also need to say something about the dates concerning when Herod the Great reigned, when Jesus was born, and when Herod died. In the timeline below I supply the dates that have been standard for a hundred years or more. According to this standard, Herod the Great was born ca. 74 BC, was appointed "king of the Jews" by the Roman senate in 40 BC, gained power after defeating Antigonus in 37 BC, and died in 4 BC. If Herod died in 4 BC, then Jesus was born in 5 or 6 BC.[1] However, not all scholars agree with this scheme. An alternate set of dates, recently well argued in a study by Andrew Steinmann, concludes that Herod was born in 71 BC, was appointed king by the Roman senate in 39 BC, defeated Antigonus in 36 BC, and died in 1 BC. In this scheme Jesus was probably born in 2 BC.[2] Among other things, this date for the birth of Jesus accords more closely with Luke's comment that Jesus began his public ministry when he was "about" thirty years old (Luke 3:23). If his ministry began in AD 28, which I think is probable, and if he was born in 2 BC, then he was indeed about thirty years of age when he commenced his ministry.

ca. 2000 BC Call of Abraham

ca. 1500 BC Call of Moses

ca. 1400 BC The Israelites enter the Promised Land.

ca. 1000 BC David captures Jerusalem.

ca. 970 BC David dies; Solomon is crowned king.

ca. 930 BC Solomon dies; kingdom splits into northern and southern kingdoms.

722–21 BC The northern kingdom (Samaria) is conquered by Assyria.

587–86 BC The southern kingdom (Judah) is conquered, Jerusalem is captured, the temple is destroyed, and many Jews are deported to Babylonia.

ca. 458 BC Ezra returns to Jerusalem.

ca. 445 BC Nehemiah returns to Jerusalem.

333–32 BC Alexander the Great sweeps through Israel, conquers the Middle East.

324 BC   Death of Aristotle, tutor of Alexander

323 BC   Death of Alexander

270 BC   Death of Epicurus (founder of Epicureanism)

ca. 265 BC   Death of Zeno (founder of Cynicism)

ca. 250 BC   Beginning of the work of translation leading to the
             Septuagint (LXX)

ca. 180 BC   Sirach (or Ecclesiasticus) was written in Hebrew, trans-
             lated into Greek approximately fifty years later.

167 BC   Desecration of the Temple by the Seleucid rul-
             er, Antiochus IV "Epiphanes" (i.e. "[Divine]
             Manifestation"), who ruled AD 175–164

164 BC   Judas Maccabeus (the "hammer") defeats General
             Lysias; Antiochus IV dies; Judas rules Judea, begins
             to enlarge borders; Hasmonean dynasty is founded;
             brothers Jonathan and Simon succeed Judas.

160 BC   Death of Judas Maccabeus; succeeded by Jonathan

142 BC   Death of Jonathan; succeeded by Simon

134 BC   Death of Simon; succeeded by John Hyrcanus I

104 BC   Death of John Hyrcanus I (son of Simon); succeeded
             by Aristobulus I

103 BC   Death of Aristobulus I (son of John Hyrcanus I); suc-
             ceeded by Alexander Jannaeus

76 BC   Death of Alexander Jannaeus (son of John Hyrcanus I)

74/71 BC   Birth of Herod (who later becomes Herod "the Great")

67 BC   Death of Alexandra (wife of Alexander Jannaeus)

67–63 BC   Aristobulus II rules briefly amidst dissension; people
             appeal to Rome.

63 BC   Pompey enters Jerusalem, thus beginning the era of
             Roman dominance. Psalms of Solomon were com-
             posed not long after this event. Hyrcanus II (son of
             Alexander Jannaeus) is made high priest.

48 BC   Julius Caesar gains mastery over Roman Empire.

44 BC	Death of Julius Caesar; Mark Antony and young Octavian (grandnephew of Caesar) avenge Caesar's murder and establish Second Triumvirate.
40/39 BC	Roman senate, at prompting of Mark Antony, declares Herod (son of Antipater II) "King of the Jews"; Parthians support Antigonus (son of Aristobulus II).
37/36 BC	Herod defeats Antigonus, last of the Hasmonean rulers, and becomes king of Israel in fact; marries Mariamne (granddaughter of Hyrcanus II); during his reign he rebuilds Jerusalem and the temple; founds several cities and fortresses.
31 BC	Octavian defeats Mark Antony and Cleopatra at Actium; becomes Roman emperor; changes name to Augustus, forgives Herod for siding with Mark Antony.
2 BC	Birth of Jesus
1 BC	Death of Herod the Great

6	Archelaus (son of Herod the Great) is deposed.
6–15	Annas (or Ananus) is appointed high priest.
14	The death of Augustus; succeeded by stepson Tiberius
18	Joseph bar Caiaphas (son-in-law of Annas) is appointed high priest.
30 or 33	Jesus is crucified.
34	Death of Herod Philip (son of Herod the Great)
36	Pontius Pilate and Joseph bar Caiaphas are removed from office.
37	Death of Tiberius; succeeded by Gaius Caligula; birth of Josephus

39	Caligula banishes Herod Antipas (son of Herod the Great) to Gaul.
41	Death of Caligula; succeeded by Claudius
44	Death of Herod Agrippa I (son of Aristobulus and Bernice, grandson of Herod the Great), after brief rule over Israel (41–44); cf. Acts 12:1–23.
ca. 50	Death of Philo of Alexandria
51–52	Tenure of Roman governor Gallio in Corinth
52–60	Tenure of the Roman governor Felix in Caesarea Maritima
ca. 53	Paul writes letter to the churches of Galatia.
54	Claudius poisoned; succeeded by Nero
ca. 55–56	Paul writes several letters to the church at Corinth.
ca. 57	Paul writes letter to the church at Rome.
60–62	Tenure of the Roman governor Festus in Caesarea Maritima
62	Ananus (son of Annas) becomes high priest, without Roman approval puts to death James the brother of Jesus; Albinus removes Ananus from office.
62–64	Tenure of the Roman governor Albinus in Caesarea
64–66	Tenure of the Roman governor Gessius Florus in Caesarea Maritima
65	Death of Seneca
66	Jewish revolt begins; governor Florus flees (or is murdered?).
ca. 67	Deaths of Peter and Paul in Rome
68	Death of Nero; succeeded by Galba
68–69	Brief reigns of Galba, Otho, and Vitellius end in murder and suicide.

69	General Vespasian, commander of the Roman forces against the Jews, is proclaimed emperor.
ca. 69	The Gospel of Mark is published.
70	Jerusalem is captured by Titus (son of Vespasian); temple is badly damaged by fire; it is later demolished.
71	Emperor Vespasian holds triumph in Rome, celebrating victory over the Jews.
73	General Silva captures Masada.
ca. 78	Josephus publishes *The Jewish War*.
79	Death of Vespasian; succeeded by his son Titus
81	Death of Titus; succeeded by brother Domitian
c. 85	Christians are excluded from some synagogues.
c. 93	Death of Agrippa II (son of Agrippa I), after ruling portions of Israel beginning in 49 (cf. Acts 25:13–26:32); Bernice was his sister.
96	Death of Domitian; succeeded by respected elderly senator Nerva
98	Death of Nerva; succeeded by adopted son Trajan; death of Josephus
ca. 112	Death of Ignatius
115	Jewish revolt in North Africa
117	Revolt put down; death of Trajan; succeeded by adopted son Hadrian
ca. 120	Tacitus publishes *The Annals*
132–135	Great Jewish revolt led by Simon ben Kosiba, dubbed "bar Kokhba"; revolt put down by Hadrian.
ca. 135	Death of Papias, author of *Expositions of the Sayings of the Lord*

138	Death of Hadrian; succeeded by Antoninus Pius
ca. 159	Death of Marcion, whose "canon" excluded the Jewish parts of the NT
ca. 165	Death of Justin Martyr, author of *First Apology*
ca. 170	Death of the Gnostic teacher Valentinus; early recognition of the New Testament canon, as reflected in the Muratorian fragment (though some date the fragment to the fourth century)
ca. 180	Publication of Greek edition of the *Gospel of Thomas*
ca. 182	Irenaeus publishes *Against Heresies*; recognizes only the Gospels of Matthew, Mark, Luke, and John.
217	The publication of *The Life of Apollonius of Tyana*, by Philostratus
ca. 220	Final editing and publication of the Mishnah
ca. 253	Death of Origen, editor of the *Hexapla* and author of numerous commentaries
325	Council of Nicea, in which "orthodox" Christology was formulated
337	Death of Constantine, first Christian emperor
339	Death of Eusebius, author of *Ecclesiastical History*
ca. 360	Production of the Coptic Gnostic books found at Nag Hammadi.
363	Council of Laodicea; discussion of which Psalms to include in canon of Scripture
373	Death of Athanasius, whose festal letter of 367 marks an important moment in the acceptance of the canon of the New Testament
381	First Council of Constantinople; convened to resolve the Arian controversy

For Further Reading

In Defense of the Christian Faith

William L. Craig, *Reasonable Faith: Christian Truth and Apologetics*, 3rd ed. (Wheaton, IL: Crossway Books, 2008).

William L. Craig and Chad Meister, eds., *God Is Great, God Is Good: Why Believing in God Is Reasonable and Responsible* (Downers Grove, IL: IVP Books, 2009).

William A. Dembski and Michael R. Licona, eds., *Evidence for God: 50 Arguments for Faith from the Bible, History, Philosophy, and Science* (Grand Rapids, MI: Baker Academic, 2010).

Timothy Keller, *The Reason for God: Belief in an Age of Scepticism* (London: Hodder & Stoughton, 2008).

J. Richard Middleton and Brian J. Walsh, *Truth Is Stranger than It Used to Be: Biblical Faith in a Postmodern Age* (Downers Grove, IL: InterVarsity, 1995).

James S. Spiegel, *The Making of an Atheist* (Chicago: Moody, 2010).

On Science and Faith

Mario Beauregard and Denyse O'Leary, *The Spiritual Brain: A Neuroscientist's Case for the Existence of the Soul* (New York: Harper, 2007).

William A. Dembski, *Intelligent Design: The Bridge between Science and Theology* (Downers Grove, IL: InterVarsity, 1999).

John C. Lennox: *God's Undertaker: Has Science Buried God?* (Oxford: Lion, 2007).

Alister McGrath, *A Fine-Tuned Universe: The Quest for God in Science and Theology* (Louisville, KY: Westminster John Knox, 2009).

Denyse O'Leary, *By Design or By Chance? The Growing Controversy on the Origins of Life in the Universe* (Minneapolis: Augsburg, 2004).

Roy A. Varghese, *The Wonder of the World: A Journey from Modern Science to the Mind of God* (Fountain Hills, AZ: Tyr, 2004).

On Archaeology

Craig A. Evans, *Jesus and His World: The Archaeological Evidence* (Louisville, KY: Westminster John Knox, 2012).

Clyde E. Fant and Mitchell G. Reddish, *A Guide to Biblical Sites in Greece and Turkey* (Oxford: Oxford University Press, 2003).

Jerome Murphy-O'Connor, *The Holy Land*, 5th ed. (Oxford: Oxford University Press, 2008).

Bargil Pixner, *Paths of the Messiah and Sites of the Early Church from Galilee to Jerusalem: Jesus and Jewish Christianity in Light of Archaeological Discoveries*, ed. R. Riesner (San Francisco: Ignatius, 2010).

On Bible Interpretation

Gordon D. Fee and Douglas Stuart, *How to Read the Bible Book by Book: A Guided Tour* (Grand Rapids, MI: Zondervan, 2002).

Robert H. Gundry, *Commentary on the New Testament: Verse-by-Verse Explanations with a Literal Translation* (Peabody, MA: Hendrickson, 2010).

Stanley E. Porter and Beth M. Stovell, eds., *Biblical Hermeneutics: Five Views* (Downers Grove, IL: InterVarsity, 2012).

Ben Witherington III, *Invitation to the New Testament: First Things* (Oxford: Oxford University Press, 2013).

N. T. Wright, *Matthew for Everyone* (London: SPCK, 2002).

On the Bible and Ethics

Paul Chamberlain, *Can We Be Good Without God? A Conversation about Truth, Morality, Culture and a Few Other Things That Matter* (Downers Grove, IL: InterVarsity, 1996).

James P. Eckman, *Biblical Ethics: Choosing Right in a World Gone Wrong* (Wheaton, IL: Crossway Books, 2004).

On the Historical Jesus

Craig A. Evans, *Fabricating Jesus: How Modern Scholars Distort the Gospels* (Downers Grove, IL: InterVarsity, 2006).

Bruce N. Fisk, *A Hitchhiker's Guide to Jesus: Reading the Gospels on the Ground* (Grand Rapids, MI: Baker Academic, 2011).

Robert H. Stein, *Jesus the Messiah: A Survey of the Life of Christ* (Downers Grove, IL: InterVarsity, 1996).

Robert H. Stein, *The Method and Message of Jesus' Teachings*, rev. ed. (Louisville, KY: Westminster John Knox, 1994).

On the Resurrection of Jesus of Nazareth

Stephen T. Davis, Daniel Kendall, and Gerald O'Collins, eds., *The Resurrection: An Interdisciplinary Symposium on the Resurrection of Jesus* (Oxford and New York: Oxford University Press, 1997).

Craig A. Evans and N. T. Wright, *Jesus, the Final Days: What Really Happened* (Louisville, KY: Westminster John Knox, 2009).

George Eldon Ladd, *I Believe in the Resurrection of Jesus* (Grand Rapids, MI: Eerdmans, 1975).

Michael R. Licona, *The Resurrection of Jesus: A New Historiographical Approach* (Downers Grove, IL: InterVarsity, 2010).

N. T. Wright, *The Resurrection of the Son of God: Christian Origins and the Question of God, Volume 3* (Minneapolis: Fortress, 2003).

Notes

Introduction

1. Among the best known is Richard Dawkins, *The God Delusion* (Boston: Houghton Mifflin, 2006). See esp. p. 51 where Dawkins describes God as "a petty, unjust . . . capriciously malevolent bully." This poorly written book has been very influential—despite being sharply criticized by several leading atheist thinkers!

2. John W. Loftus, "The Bible and the Christian Tradition are Irrelevant," Debunking Christianity (blog), November 16, 2007, http://debunkingchristianity.blogspot.com/2007/11/bible-and-christian-tradition-are.html. The second quote is from a comment by the author to his blog post.

3. Hilary Beaumont, "Is There Any Room for God in Government?," *Chronicle Herald* (Halifax, Nova Scotia), last updated January 5, 2013, http://thechronicleherald.ca/religion/373791-is-there-any-room-for-god-in-government.

Chapter 1: What Is the Bible, Really?

1. For an in-depth study of the contents and development of the Bible, see Lee Martin McDonald, *Formation of the Bible: The Story of the Church's Canon* (Peabody, MA: Hendrickson, 2012).

2. For an introduction to the books of the Apocrypha, see David A. deSilva, *Introducing the Apocrypha: Message, Context, and Significance* (Grand Rapids, MI: Baker, 2002).

3. For a solid introduction and survey of the literature of the Old Testament, see Raymond B. Dillard and Tremper Longman III, *An Introduction to the Old Testament* (Grand Rapids, MI: Zondervan, 1994).

4. For a reliable introduction and survey of the New Testament, see David A. deSilva, *An Introduction to the New Testament: Contexts, Methods, and Ministry Formation* (Downers Grove, IL: InterVarsity, 2004).

5. I recommend Gordon D. Fee and Douglas Stuart, *How to Read the Bible Book by Book: A Guided Tour* (Grand Rapids, MI: Zondervan, 2002).

6. Perhaps the best-known book making this claim is B. D. Ehrman, *Misquoting Jesus: The Story Behind Who Changed the Bible and Why* (New York: HarperSanFrancisco, 2005).

7. The Dead Sea Scrolls are ancient Jewish scrolls that were found near Qumran on the northwest shore of the Dead Sea.

8. The evidence is presented clearly and convincingly in F. F. Bruce, *The New Testament Documents: Are They Reliable?* 6th ed. (Downers Grove, IL: InterVarsity, 2003).

9. Tertullian, *Prescription against Heresies*, chapter 36. I discuss this important evidence in some detail in my essay, "How Long Were Late Antique Books in Use? Possible Implications for New Testament Textual Criticism," *Bulletin for Biblical Research* 25, no. 1 (2015): 23–37.

10. Josephus also discusses John the Baptist, and what he says complements what the Gospels say about this important figure. Indeed, Josephus talks about Jesus, and what he says agrees in broad outline with the New Testament Gospels.

11. This important point is made by the distinguished New Testament scholar E. P. Sanders, in his influential book, *Jesus and Judaism* (London: SCM, 1985), 164: "The miracles attracted the crowds. . . . If it is true that large crowds surrounded him in Galilee, it was probably more because of his ability to heal and exorcize than anything else."

Chapter 2: What's the Bible Saying, Really?

1. The Promised Land of Canaan runs from Sinai in the south to the southern boundary of Lebanon in the north and from the Jordan River to the east to the Mediterranean Sea to the west.

2. On the Gospels as examples of ancient biography, see Richard A. Burridge, *What Are the Gospels? A Comparison with Graeco-Roman Biography,* 2nd ed. (Grand Rapids, MI: Eerdmans, 2004).

3. See Albert Pietersma and Benjamin G. Wright, eds., *A New English Translation of the Septuagint and the Other Translations Traditionally Included under That Title* (Oxford: Oxford University Press, 2007). Another English version is available in the Eastern / Greek Orthodox Bible (EOB), published in 2011.

4. Most of these books of the Apocrypha are available in Greek. Hebrew fragments of some of them have been recovered in the last century or so (such as Tobit, Ecclesiasticus, and Psalm 151).

Chapter 3: Why Do We Need a Creation Story?

1. As in the case of Bart Ehrman. See his book, *God's Problem: How the Bible Fails to answer our Most Important Question—Why We Suffer* (New York: HarperOne, 2008). Christian thinkers and theologians who have pondered this important question (sometimes referred to as theodicy, "divine justice") believe that the Bible in fact does answer this question. For reviews that criticize Ehrman's book, see Chris Hedges, "A Hollow Agnosticism," *Harvard Divinity Bulletin* 36, no. 2 (Spring 2008); J. C. Howell, in *Charlotte Observer,* March 16, 2008. See the discussion of God and suffering in Timothy Keller, *The Reason for God: Belief in an Age of Scepticism* (London: Hodder & Stoughton, 2008), 22–34.

2. As a teenager Richard Dawkins wrongly believed that science and belief in God were at odds and that one had to be accepted and the other rejected. This is, alas, a false dichotomy. Rightly understood, the Bible and science complement one another. Scientists who are atheists are atheists usually for reasons that have nothing to do with science. See Keller, *Reason for God*, 84–96.

3. This theory was usually called the "Steady State" hypothesis.

4. The implications of the Big Bang are so troubling for some committed atheists that they try to salvage the Steady State belief, either by redefining "nothing" (i.e., as something

after all) or by hypothesizing an endless number of failed universes that preceded our own (called the multiverse hypothesis). The first option is nonsense. The second is pure science fiction. Both options are attempts to recover some form of the discredited Steady State hypothesis.

5. For an excellent treatment of the formation of the universe and the uniqueness of our solar system and our planet, see Guillermo Gonzalez and Jay W. Richards, *The Privileged Planet: How Our Place in the Cosmos is Designed for Discovery* (Washington, DC: Regnery, 2004). See also William A. Dembski, *The Design Inference: Eliminating Chance through Small Probabilities* (Cambridge: Cambridge University Press, 1998); William A. Dembski, *No Free Lunch: Why Specified Complexity Cannot be Purchased without Intelligence* (Lanham, MD: Rowman & Littlefield, 2002); Denyse O'Leary, *By Design or By Chance? The Growing Controversy on the Origins of Life in the Universe* (Minneapolis: Augsburg, 2004); and Roy A. Varghese, *The Wonder of the World: A Journey from Modern Science to the Mind of God* (Fountain Hills, AZ: Tyr, 2004).

6. James B. Pritchard, *Ancient Near Eastern Texts Relating to the Old Testament* (Princeton: Princeton University Press, 1969), 6.

7. Pritchard, *Ancient Near Eastern Texts*, 60–61.

8. Ancient Indian and Chinese creation stories are similar to those of the ancient Near East. For further inquiry, see David A. Leeming and Margaret Adams, eds., *A Dictionary of Creation Myths* (Oxford: Oxford University Press, 1994); David A. Leeming, *Creation Myths of the World*, 2nd ed. (Santa Barbara, CA: ABC-CLIO, 2010).

9. Gonzalez and Richards, *The Privileged Planet*, 133–36.

10. Richard Dawkins senses this problem, suggesting that if chance cannot explain the origin of life on earth, then perhaps aliens seeded the earth with life. This of course does not solve the problem; it simply tries to explain a mystery with another mystery—and a highly unlikely one at that. Dawkins made this comment on the National Public Radio program *Fresh Air*, March 27, 2007. For another important work that challenges mere chance as an explanation of our world, see William A. Dembski, *Signs of Intelligence: Understanding Intelligent Design* (Grand Rapids, MI: Brazos, 2001).

11. Asao Fujiyama et al., "Construction and Analysis of a Human-Chimpanzee Comparative Clone Map," *Science* 295, no. 5552 (January 2002): 131–34; Pascal Gagneux and Ajit Varki, "Genetic Differences between Humans and Great Apes," *Molecular Phylogenetics and Evolution* 18, no. 1 (January 2001): 2–13. Some scientists bump up the percentage of agreement between humans and apes to 98 percent.

12. For more on this important point, see John Eccles and Daniel N. Robinson, *The Wonder of Being Human: Our Brain and Our Mind* (New York: Free Press, 1984), 104–13; Mario Beauregard and Denyse O'Leary, *The Spiritual Brain: A Neuroscientist's Case for the Existence of the Soul* (New York: Harper, 2007), 13–19.

13. See the especially helpful book by Beauregard and O'Leary, *The Spiritual Brain*. One should also consult the classic work by Eccles and Robinson, *The Wonder of Being Human*, as well as the more recent and highly technical collection of studies, Edward F. Kelly, Emily Williams Kelly et al., *Irreducible Mind: Toward a Psychology for the 21st*

Century (Lanham, MD: Rowman & Littlefield, 2007). Ongoing scientific research has demolished theories of materialism and physicalism.

14. For studies of science and faith, I recommend the following books by Alister McGrath: *Science and Religion: An Introduction* (Oxford: Blackwell, 1998); *A Scientific Theology*, 3 vols. (Grand Rapids, MI: Eerdmans, 2001–2003); and *A Fine-Tuned Universe: The Quest for God in Science and Theology* (Louisville, KY: Westminster John Knox, 2009). I also recommend the following books by John C. Lennox: *God's Undertaker: Has Science Buried God?* (Oxford: Lion, 2007); *Gunning for God: Why the New Atheists are Missing the Target* (Oxford: Lion, 2011). See also William A. Dembski, *Intelligent Design: The Bridge between Science and Theology* (Downers Grove, IL: InterVarsity, 1999).

15. See Antony Flew, *There Is a God: How the World's Most Notorious Atheist Changed His Mind* (New York: HarperOne, 2007). Flew is to be commended for his honesty and integrity. After sixty years of atheism he changed his mind in 2004. In the book that appeared in 2007 he explains why he did. Flew died in 2010. Many atheists do not want there to be a God, whatever the evidence suggests. On this important aspect of the debate, see James S. Spiegel, *The Making of an Atheist* (Chicago: Moody, 2010). Spiegel quotes atheist philosopher Thomas Nagel, who says: "I want atheism to be true and am made uneasy by the fact that some of the most intelligent and well-informed people I know are religious believers. It isn't just that I don't believe in God, and, naturally, hope that I'm right about my belief. It's that I hope there is no God! I don't want there to be a God; I don't want the universe to be like that" (p. 11). See Thomas Nagel, *The Last Word* (New York: Oxford University Press, 1997), 130.

16. The popular notion of "artificial intelligence" has been widely debunked. See John R. Searle, *Mind: A Brief Introduction* (Oxford: Oxford University Press, 2004), 74; Beauregard and O'Leary, *Spiritual Brain*, 19–23; Ari N. Schulman, "Why Minds Are Not Like Computers," *The New Atlantis: A Journal of Technology & Society* (Winter 2009), http://www.thenewatlantis.com/publications/why-minds-are-not-like-computers. Schulman speaks of artificial intelligence as a myth. He is quite correct, for no computer possesses consciousness. Without consciousness there can hardly be intelligence in the true sense of the word. A computer functions; it does not think. And a computer's functionality is no better than the computer's programming.

17. Francis S. Collins, *The Language of God: A Scientist Presents Evidence for Belief* (New York: Free Press, 2006). It is not enough to have the genetic information; *it has to be in the proper sequence*, as surely as words must be in their proper sequence.

18. See the discussion in Peter Enns, *The Evolution of Adam: What the Bible Does and Doesn't Say about Human Origins* (Grand Rapids, MI: Brazos, 2012). The major challenge in interpreting the stories about Adam and Eve, Cain and Abel, Noah and the Flood, and the Tower of Babel is in determining the nature of this literature. Not everything in the Bible is "history" in the way we understand history today. Truth is often conveyed in parables, as seen, for example, in the many parables uttered by Jesus.

19. The story of God's prevention of Abraham's sacrifice of Isaac may also implicitly condemn human sacrifice, which was practiced in the ancient Near East. In contrast to the pagan gods, the God of Abraham does not require humans to offer up their children.

20. Sheol was the place of the dead—righteous and unrighteous alike.

21. On levirate marriage, see Deuteronomy 25:5. The purpose of this custom was to protect the childless widow, guaranteeing her place in the family of her late husband. The levirate practice lies behind the question that the Sadducees posed to Jesus in Matthew 22:23–33. In later times the practice, along with polygamy itself, was discontinued.

22. Readers should know that the patriarchal stories are selective, compressed, and not always in strict chronological sequence.

Chapter 4: Isn't the Bible Just Rules and Negative Talk?

1. Augustine, *Confessions* 1.1.1.

2. The Aramaic text that I have cited is called Targum, which means "translation." There are three complete Aramaic translations/paraphrases of the books of Moses. The one I have quoted is called Neofiti. Genesis 49:10 is quoted in one of the Dead Sea Scrolls (4Q252 frag. 5), which dates to the first century BC. In this scroll the "scepter" of Judah is understood as the "Righteous Messiah, the Branch of David."

3. Here I have followed the Targum that is known as Onqelos. Instead of "Messiah," the Neofiti Targum paraphrases "Redeemer and Ruler."

4. Numbers 24:17 is applied to the awaited Messiah in the Blessings Scroll (1QSb 5:27–28), in a passage that outlines the blessings that are to be pronounced on the messianic Prince when he comes to Israel. Numbers 24:17–19 also appears in the famous War Scroll (1QM 11:6–7) and in a collection of prophecies (4Q175 1:9–13). First-century Jewish historian Josephus applies Numbers 24:17 to the Roman general Vespasian after his victory over the Jewish people and his crowning as emperor in AD 69. See Josephus, *Jewish Wars* 6.312–13. Even Roman writers and historians knew of this Jewish oracle and how it had come to be understood as fulfilled in Vespasian. See Tacitus, *Histories* 5; Suetonius, *Vespasian* 4, 5.

5. For a collection of recent studies of the Ten Commandments, see Jeffrey P. Greenman and Timothy Larsen, eds., *The Decalogue through the Centuries: From the Hebrew Scriptures to Benedict XVI* (Louisville, KY: Westminster John Knox, 2012).

6. It is estimated that fifty million abortions have taken place in the United States since the fateful Supreme Court decision in *Roe v. Wade* in 1973.

7. For more on this important topic, I recommend Alvin J. Schmidt, *How Christianity Changed the World* (Grand Rapids, MI: Zondervan, 2004); Jonathan Hill, *What Has Christianity Ever Done for Us? How It Shaped the Modern World* (Downers Grove, IL: InterVarsity, 2005). You may also want to see Rodney Stark, *The Victory of Reason: How Christianity Led to Freedom, Capitalism, and Western Success* (New York: Random House, 2005).

8. Here one thinks of Abigail's husband Nabal, whose Hebrew name means "foolish." As Abigail explained to King David, her husband had lived up to the meaning of his name. See 1 Samuel 25:3, 25, 39.

9. The Law of Moses generously allowed the poor to glean from the fields of their more prosperous neighbors. See Deuteronomy 24:19–22.

10. Another descendant in the line of Boaz and David would use this language. Grieved over the city of Jerusalem, Jesus said: "O Jerusalem, Jerusalem . . . How often would I have gathered your children together as a hen gathers her brood under her wings . . . " (Matthew 23:37; Luke 13:34).

11. Parts of 2 Samuel 7 are quoted in one of the Dead Sea Scrolls in a way that suggests that the prophecy of Nathan was understood as pertaining to the Messiah. See 1Q174 2:19–3:13. The Greek translation of 2 Samuel 7 also seems to understand the prophecy as in reference to the anticipated Messiah.

Chapter 5: What's the Bright Side of the Bible?

1. Richard Dawkins, *River out of Eden: A Darwinian View of Life* (New York: Basic Books, 1995), 133.

2. Bertrand Russell, *Why I Am Not a Christian*, ed. Paul Edwards (New York: Simon & Schuster, 1957), 107.

3. Thomas Nagel, *What Does It All Mean? A Very Short Introduction to Philosophy* (New York: Oxford, 1987), 100.

4. It is important to remark that not all who claim to be atheists think and act in ways that are consistent with atheism. Many atheists speak of morality and concepts of right and wrong. But if there is no God, there really are no grounds for morals. Some atheists rightly recognize this. This is why Dawkins says there is "no evil and no good, nothing but blind, pitiless indifference." For further discussion of this important topic, see Paul Chamberlain, *Can We Be Good without God?: A Conversation about Truth, Morality, Culture, and a Few Other Things That Matter* (Downers Grove, IL: InterVarsity, 1996).

5. Billy Graham, *Peace with God*, rev. ed. (Waco, TX: Word Books, 1984).

Chapter 7: Where Did Jesus Come From and What Did He Teach?

1. Translation based on Michael O. Wise, Martin G. Abegg, Jr., and Edward M. Cook, *The Dead Sea Scrolls: A New Translation* (San Francisco: HarperCollins, 1996), 421. Even with restorations there are still gaps in the text.

2. We also think of Jesus commanding the storm to cease (Mark 4:35–41), which prompts the disciples to ask: "Who then is this, that even the wind and the sea obey him?" (Mark 4:41).

3. Josephus, *Antiquities* 4.242–43.

4. From the Babylonian Talmud, tractate *Berakoth* ("Blessings").

5. This interpretation is found in *Sipre Deuteronomy* §297 (commenting on Deuteronomy 26:1–2] and *Mekilta*, commenting on Exodus 23:19 (in tractate *Kaspa* section §5).

6. Josephus, *Jewish War* 6.300–309.

Chapter 8: Does It Matter That People Hear about Jesus?

1. The charge that the risen Jesus gave his disciples, that they should preach the good news and teach (see Matthew 28:18–20), is called the Great Commission.

2. Among others, see Irenaeus, *Against Heresies* 2.6.2 (*c.* 180 CE). The name of Jesus is invoked in pagan magical texts (e.g., *Greek Magical Papyrus* IV.3007–86): "I adjure you

by the name of the God of the Hebrews—Jesus!"

3. The quotation comes from David Aikman, *Jesus in Beijing: How Christianity Is Transforming China and Changing the Global Balance of Power* (Washington, DC: Regnery, 2003), 5. I recommend the following books by Rodney Stark: *One True God: Historical Consequences of Monotheism* (Princeton: Princeton University Press, 2001); *The Victory of Reason: How Christianity Led to Freedom, Capitalism, and Western Success* (New York: Random House, 2005); and *Cities of God: The Real Story of How Christianity Became an Urban Movement and Conquered Rome* (San Francisco: HarperSanFrancisco, 2006). See also Jonathan Hill, *What Has Christianity Ever Done for Us? How It Shaped the Modern World* (Downers Grove, IL: InterVarsity, 2005).

4. See data made available on the Focus Prison Ministries and Prison Fellowship International websites.

5. One of these coins is on display at the Ashmolean Museum in Oxford. I viewed it in December 2009. On the early history of the Jesus movement, I invite readers to see my book, *From Jesus to the Church: The First Christian Generation* (Louisville, KY: Westminister John Knox, 2014).

6. See the accounts in Eusebius, *Ecclesiastical History* 10.5; Lactantius, *The Deaths of the Persecutors* 48. The letter that Constantine issued has been traditionally called the "Edict of Milan," though it was not in fact an edict.

7. Readers of English heritage will want to see F. F. Bruce, *The Spreading Flame: The Rise and Progress of Christianity from its First Beginnings to the Conversion of the English* (London: Paternoster, 1958; repr. Grand Rapids, MI: Eerdmans, 1995). Although dated, Williston Walker's *A History of the Christian Church* (New York: Scribner's Sons, 1970) remains a classic.

8. It is projected that by 2020 there will be 2.6 billion Christians worldwide. See Jessica Martínez, "Study: 2.6 Billion of World Population Expected to Be Christian by 2020," *Christian Post*, July 19, 2013, http://www.christianpost.com/news/study-2-6-billion-of-world-population-expected-to-be-christian-by-2020-100402/.

Chapter 9: Why Do We Need to Hear about the End of the World?

1. As reported a few years ago. See Rachel Zoll, "Study: Christian population shifts from Europe," *Gainesville (FL) Guardian*, December 22, 2011, http://www.gainesville.com/article/20111222/GUARDIAN/111229921.

2. On this important topic, see Jerry Johnston, *Why They Die: Curing the Death Wish in Our Kids* (Burlington, Ontario: Crossroads, 2012).

Chapter 10: How Do We Know What the Bible Means?

1. For example, Tom Wright, *Matthew for Everyone* 2 vols. (Louisville, KY: Westminster John Knox, 2004). Professor Wright has completed the entire New Testament.

2. Gordon D. Fee and Douglas Stuart, *How to Read the Bible Book by Book: A Guided Tour* (Grand Rapids, MI: Zondervan, 2014); Fee and Stuart, *How to Read the Bible for All Its Worth* (Grand Rapids, MI: Zondervan, 2014).

Chapter 11: How Should We Understand the Violence and Anger in the Bible?

1. Samuel Sandmel, *Anti-Semitism in the New Testament?* (Philadelphia: Fortress, 1978), 160.

2. For an introduction and survey of the scrolls, see Craig A. Evans, *Holman QuickSource Guide to the Dead Sea Scrolls* (Nashville: B&H, 2010).

3. 1QHa is in reference to the Hymns Scroll (Hebrew: *Hodayot*) found in Cave 1 of Qumran, near the Dead Sea. Cave 1 was discovered we believe in 1947 and was the first of eleven caves containing scrolls discovered in the region over a decade or so. The translation is based on Wise, Abegg, and Cook, *The Dead Sea Scrolls*, 95–96.

4. 1QS is in reference to the Rule of the Community scroll (Hebrew: *Serek haYahad*). The translation based on Wise, Abegg, and Cook, *The Dead Sea Scrolls*, 130. Like the Hymn Scroll the Rule Scroll was also found in Cave 1 of Qumran.

5. These colorful epithets are found in CD 8:12; 1QpHab 1:13; 8:8; 9:9; 10:9; 10:17–11:1; 11:4.

Chapter 12: What Discoveries Assure Us the Bible Is True?

1. Ron S. Hendel, "Giants at Jericho," *Biblical Archaeology Review* 35, no. 2 (March/April 2009): 20, 66, with quotation from p. 20.

2. For an assessment of some of the most important manuscript and archaeological discoveries that in fact do support the Bible, especially relating to the New Testament writings, see F. F. Bruce, *The New Testament Documents: Are They Reliable?* 6th ed. (Downers Grove, IL: InterVarsity, 2003); Craig A. Evans, *Jesus and His World: The Archaeological Evidence* (Louisville, KY: Westminster John Knox, 2012).

3. Translation adapted from E. A. W. Budge, *The Rosetta Stone in the British Museum* (London: Religious Tract Society, 1929), 51–52.

4. See A. F. Rainey, "Shasu or Habiru: Who were the Early Israelites?" *Biblical Archaeology Review* 34, no. 6 (November/December 2008): 51–55.

5. See F. J. Yurco, "3,200-Year-Old Picture of Israelites Found in Egypt," *Biblical Archaeology Review* 16, no. 5 (September/October 1990): 20–38; H. S. Shanks, "When Did Ancient Israel Begin? New Hieroglyphic Inscription May Date Israel's Ethnogenesis 200 Years Earlier Than You Thought," *Biblical Archaeology Review* 38, no. 1 (January/February 2012): 59–62, 67.

6. Translation based on Pritchard, *Ancient Near Eastern Texts*, 287–88.

7. For a recent study that revisits Sennacherib's invasion of Judah, see M. Cogan, "Sennacherib's Siege of Jerusalem: Once or Twice?" *Biblical Archaeology Review* 27, no. 1 (January/February 2001): 40–45, 69.

8. See A. Biran, " 'David' Found at Dan," *Biblical Archaeology Review* 20, no. 2 (March/April 1994): 26–39; A. Lemaire, "The Tel Dan Stela as a Piece of Royal Historiography," *Journal for the Study of the Old Testament* 23, no. 81 (December 1998): 3–14. The words "House of David" may also appear in line 31 of the famous Mesha Inscription, which dates to ca. 840 BC and was found in 1868. The inscription

outlines Mesha's conflicts with Israel (see 2 Kings 3:4–27). (Mesha was king of Moab.) For discussion, see A. Lemaire, "'House of David' Restored in Moabite Inscription," *Biblical Archaeology Review* 20, no. 3 (May/June 1994): 30–37. The Mesha Inscription is housed in the Louvre in Paris.

9. David is only one of some fifty biblical figures who have been confirmed by archaeology. See Lawrence Mykytiuk, "Archaeology Confirms 50 Real People in the Bible," *Biblical Archaeology Review* 40, no. 2 (March/April 2014): 42–50, 68. There are several other possible candidates.

10. See Eilat Mazar, "Did I Find King David's Palace?" *Biblical Archaeology Review* 32, no. 1 (January/February 2006): 16–27; A. Faust, "Did Eilat Mazar Find David's Palace?" *Biblical Archaeology Review* 38, no. 5 (September/October 2012): 47–52, 70. For additional support of Mazar's findings, see N. Na'aman, "The Interchange between Bible and Archaeology: The Case of David's Palace and the Millo," *Biblical Archaeology Review* 40, no. 1 (January/February 2014): 57–61, 68–69. For an overview of excavations relating to Jerusalem in the 10th century BC, see H. S. Shanks, "Jerusalem Roundup," *Biblical Archaeology Review* 37, no. 2 (March/April 2011): 35–45.

11. See S. J. Andrews, "The Oldest Attested Hebrew Scriptures and the Khirbet Qeiyafa Inscription," in Craig A. Evans, ed., *The World of Jesus and the Early Church: Identity and Interpretation in the Early Communities of Faith* (Peabody, MA: Hendrickson, 2011), 153–68; C. A. Rollston, "What's the Oldest Hebrew Inscription?" *Biblical Archaeology Review* 38, no. 3 (May/June 2012): 32–40, 66, 68.

12. Tacitus, *Annals* 15.44.

13. See A. H. M. Jones, *Studies in Roman Government and Law* (Oxford: Blackwell, 1960), 117–25. For an early report concerning the "Pilate Inscription," see Jerry Vardaman, "A New Inscription which Mentions Pilate as 'Prefect,'" *Journal of Biblical Literature* 81 (1962): 70–71. The Latin inscription reads: "[Pon]tius Pilatus praefectus Iudaeae."

14. See Franz Cumont, "Un réscrit imperial sur la violation de sepulture," *Revue Historique* 163 (1930): 341–66 + plate.

15. For further discussion, see P. W. van der Horst, *Ancient Jewish Epitaphs: An Introductory Survey of a Millennium of Jewish Funerary Epigraphy (300 BCE – 700 CE)* (Kampen: Kok Pharos, 1991), 159–60.

16. See M. Avi-Jonah, "A List of Priestly Courses from Caesarea," *Israel Exploration Journal* 12 (1962): 137–39 + plate.

17. Josephus, *Antiquities* 18.35.

18. Josephus, *Antiquities* 18.95.

19. See Z. Greenhut, "The Caiaphas Tomb in North Talpiyot, Jerusalem," in *Ancient Jerusalem Revealed Archaeology in the Holy City*, ed. Hillel Geva (Jerusalem: Israel Exploration Society, 1994), 219–22.

20. For study of the Miriam Ossuary, see Boaz Zissu and Yuval Goren, "The Ossuary of 'Miriam Daughter of Yeshua Son of Caiaphas, Priests [of] Ma'aziah from Beth 'Imri'," *Israel Exploration Journal* 61, no. 1 (2011): 74–95; Richard Bauckham, "The Caiaphas Family," *Journal for the Study of the Historical Jesus* 10, no. 1 (2012): 3–31.

21. See Craig A. Evans, *Jesus and the Ossuaries* (Waco, TX: Baylor University Press, 2003), 112–22. For a study of James the brother of Jesus that takes into account the potential significance of the James Ossuary, see Hershel S. Shanks and Ben Witherington III, *The Brother of Jesus: The Dramatic Story and Meaning of the First Archaeological Link to Jesus and His Family* (San Francisco: HarperSanFrancisco, 2003).

22. See Y. Yadin, "Epigraphy and Crucifixion," *Israel Exploration Journal* 23, no. 1 (1973): 18–22 + plate; Joseph Zias and Eliezer Sekeles, "The Crucified Man from Giv'at ha-Mivtar: A Reappraisal," *Israel Exploration Journal* 35, no. 1 (1985): 22–27.

23. For a very interesting report of the discovery and study of the Shroud Tomb, see Shimon Gibson, *The Final Days of Jesus: The Archaeological Evidence* (New York: HarperOne, 2009), 138–47.

24. Josephus, *Antiquities* 20.200–201.

25. For a preliminary study of the Magdala synagogue, see Jürgen K. Zangenberg, "Archaeological News from the Galilee: Tiberias, Magdala, and Rural Galilee," *Early Christianity* 1 (2010), 471–484, esp. 475–77; Joey Corbett, "New Synagogue Excavations in Israel and Beyond," *Biblical Archaeology Review* 37, no. 4 (July/August 2011): 52–59. Whether this site should be identified as Magdala is still under review.

26. See Shelley Wachsmann, *The Sea of Galilee Boat: A 2000-Year-Old Discovery from the Sea of Legends* (Cambridge, MA: Perseus, 2000).

27. For a study of the shape of the cross, as well as the practice of crucifixion, see Gunnar Samuelsson, *Crucifixion in Antiquity*, 2nd ed. (Tübingen: Mohr Siebeck, 2013); John Granger Cook, *Crucifixion in the Mediterranean World* (Tübingen: Mohr Siebeck, 2014).

28. Josephus, *Jewish Wars* 5.193–94; see also Josephus, *Antiquities* 12.145.

29. For an early study, see W. F. Albright, "A Biblical Fragment from the Maccabean Age: The Nash Papyrus," *Journal of Biblical Literature* 56, no. 3 (September 1937): 145–76. For a recent study, see Marvin A. Sweeney, "The Nash Papyrus—Preview of Coming Attractions," *Biblical Archaeology Review* 36, no. 4 (July/August 2010): 43–48, 77.

30. For an introduction to the Dead Sea Scrolls, one may wish to see my book, *Holman QuickSource Guide to the Dead Sea Scrolls* (Nashville: B&H, 2010).

Chapter 13: Who Did What and When Did It Happen?

1. For a clear statement of the factors that go into some of these standard dates, see Harold W. Hoehner, *Chronological Aspects of the Life of Christ* (Grand Rapids, MI: Zondervan, 1977), 11–27.

2. Andrew E. Steinmann, "When Did Herod the Great Reign?" *Novum Testamentum* 51 (2009), 1–29. The principal reason we have two conflicting sets of dates is because of inconsistency in the dates provided by Josephus, the first-century Jewish historian.

About the Author

CRAIG A. EVANS is Payzant Distinguished Professor of New Testament at Acadia Divinity College and Acadia University. Before his appointment at Acadia in 2002 he taught for twenty-one years at Trinity Western University, where he founded the Dead Sea Scrolls Institute. He received a B.A. from Claremont McKenna College, M.Div. from Western Seminary, M.A. and Ph.D. from Claremont Graduate University, and D.Habil. from Károli Gáspár Református University in Budapest.

He has served as editor-in-chief of the *Bulletin for Biblical Research* and has published more than five hundred scholarly books, articles, and reviews. Professor Evans has lectured in universities and museums around the world and has appeared in news programs and documentaries that have aired on BBC, Discovery Channel, History Channel, National Geographic Channel, *CBS Sunday Morning,* and *Dateline NBC.* Professor Evans and his wife, Ginny, live in Kentville, Nova Scotia, and have two grown daughters and a grandson.

WORTHY®

PUBLISHING

If you enjoyed this book, will you consider sharing the message with others?

- Mention the book in a Facebook post, Twitter update, Pinterest pin, blog post, or upload a picture through Instagram.

- Recommend this book to those in your small group, book club, workplace, and classes.

- Head over to facebook.com/worthypublishing, "LIKE" the page, and post a comment as to what you enjoyed the most.

- Tweet "I recommend reading #GodSpeaks by Dr. Craig Evans// @worthypub"

- Pick up a copy for someone you know who would be challenged and encouraged by this message.

- Write a book review online.

You can subscribe to Worthy Publishing's newsletter at worthypublishing.com.

WORTHY PUBLISHING
FACEBOOK PAGE

WORTHY PUBLISHING
WEBSITE